REVISED
EDITION

A fashion guide for the fuller figure . . .

SEW BIG!™

by Marilyn Thelen

Copyright © 1980 Palmer/Pletsch Associates.
Revised edition copyright © 1981 Palmer/Pletsch Associates.
Fourth printing
Published by Palmer/Pletsch Associates,
Portland, Oregon, U.S.A.

Design and Production by Brown/Wisner, Eugene, Oregon.
Photography by Carol Day (or as credited).
Illustration by Alan Stephenson and Brown/Wisner.
Printed by The Irwin-Hodson Company, Portland, Oregon.

SEW BIG™ Pending   ISBN 0-935278-06-0

Marilyn Thelen is a Home Economics graduate (Oregon State University) with 20 years experience in the fashion field. In 1981, she joined McCall Pattern Company acting as spokesperson for their 14PLUS large-size program. Thelen then became the editor of "It's Me", a national large-size fashion magazine and in 1985, she moved to the Tribute Companies to design a large-size dress line bearing her name, PREMIER ROW BY MARILYN THELEN. For the past five years, she has traveled nationwide publicizing large-size fashion via fashion shows, seminars and media appearances. Thelen is a member of The Fashion Group and Women in Communications, both national organizations for women in business.

Author's Note;

I originally wrote SEW BIG to give basic fashion information to women my size. At the time, we had few fashion choices. Granted the large-size fashion market has evolved, but we still have few role-models once a person outgrows our size 10 society. To recreate fashion's seasonal affects, larger women need to develop proficiency in shopping, altering and home sewing. Re-reading SEW BIG, I find that its content is still applicable. When Pati, Susan and I revised it in 1981, we included more material from teachers, readers and manufacturers to create a "how to" book that would teach the reader the basics. My experience has taught me that the world of fashion is not closed to anyone who is properly motivated. I don't feel that I've found any great answers, but I feel that if I can find ways to dress the way I want to, everyone can. And that's my message. Fashion is for fun and it's for everyone, regardless of size.

Table of Contents

Table of Contents

"When my children were small,
they would crawl up on my lap and ask,
"How big am I?" I would always
answer "SOOO BIG!!"

CHAPTER ONE
Getting Acquainted

When my children were small, they would crawl up on my lap, stretch their arms high in the air, and ask, "How big am I?" I would always answer, "Sooo Big!"

They wanted to be BIG, because compared to the rest of their world, they felt small.

We only feel BIG when we compare ourselves to someone smaller. If we look in the mirror, we see our own body shape, and that's the figure we have to dress. To look attractive, we need to know how to create optical illusions, using clothes as our camouflage. And this applies whether we are 6 feet, size 16; or a 5-foot size 22.

The fashion world has created a tall-thin stereotype of the female figure, when actually size has nothing to do with creating a fashionable appearance. (I've seen some pretty dowdy size 10's!)

We aren't always interested in duplicating fashion looks, but rather in adapting trends that compliment our individual shape and taste. It's a challenge. I've learned that proportion, silhouette and scale all have to be taken into consideration when we look at design.

I can honestly say that there has never been a fashion look that I haven't been able to convert . . . well, maybe I skipped HOT PANTS! I am 5 feet 8 inches tall and have worn every size from a 14 to a 22, counting tops and bottoms. You can see from the cover photo that I feel fashion is fun.

This book is designed to explain the techniques of fashionable wardrobe planning, pattern and fabric selection, and accessorization and coordination that compliment the larger silhouette. I've focused on sewing techniques and alterations that will increase the range of clothing available. I'm going to talk about the tricks of buying patterns, fabrics, and ready-to-wear that will allow you to dress in fashion no matter what size you wear.

Of course, my experience working as a fabric representative for a national manufacturer and as a fashion journalist *(California Apparel News* and *Christian Science Monitor)* has given my eyes and ears lots of input during the last 15 years. I've covered apparel markets, sometimes looking at hundreds of collections in a single day. At retail, I've managed in-store promotions for both men's and women's fashions, so I know how merchandising works. And I've written publicity for clothing manufacturers over the years, which gives me a good idea of their consumer message. I believe exposure gives everyone expanded awareness. Let's face it; we don't change our perspective until we're inspired. Sometimes we need new information to develop new ideas and attitudes.

We are going to learn to sew and shop with new eyes. It's time to get with it! Why should everyone else look like a million dollars, while we look like 2 cents? Remember, SIZE is not an obstacle in playing the fashion game. And fashion is like any other game. Sometimes you'll win . . . sometimes you'll lose. Sometimes, you'll experience frustration. But winning makes the game exciting, and the result is looking terrific!

Basically, SEW BIG is a concept . . . a way to think of yourself. I suggest that you read completely through the book, before you begin to sew, just as you would read a novel.

CHAPTER TWO

Creating Fashion Awareness

Once I read a book titled, *I Can Tell By Your Outfit.* How true! Too often, our first impressions are based on appearance, rather than on a person's inner qualities.

There's no doubt that our appearance affects others. And if we are truthful, it affects the attitude that we have about ourselves, too.

Add Spice to Your Life

Our whole life we have been bombarded with dictums. Do this . . . do that! Wear this . . . wear that! Why, then would we want to step into the fashion parade, especially when the odds seem to be against our making the grade? Because dressing fashionably adds spice to life. It's fun to wear great-looking clothes.

The Western look can easily be adapted to the larger figure. Here is a feminized version of the classic shirt dress in denim, worn with western boots.

Start a Fashion File

We want to dress fashionably, but often we don't have the knack. So how can a person create "fashion consciousness"? Simply by doing some homework. To begin, start a FASHION FILE. Everyone's file will take on its own individual shape. Mine consists of pictures and articles that are tacked up by my sewing machine, pinned up on my bulletin board, and stuffed into manila folders.

Study Fashion Magazines

One way that reference material is gathered is by reading fashion and fashion/sewing magazines. You can subscribe, buy only the issues you want, or go to the library and copy any material that you find interesting. This exercise is meant to train your fashion eye to see detail. As you look through the magazines, take note of one thing at a time.

For example, look at necklines, making a record of the ones that you think would look good on you. If you aren't sure about the style, later take a piece of fabric and duplicate the design by draping it about your neckline, remembering that different fabric weights will affect the design.

Read Fashion Advertisements

When you look at newspapers and magazines, don't overlook the advertising. Often, the season's strongest trend stories are told in the ads. For example, when fashion turns to western wear, ads are created to give us the top-to-bottom look . . . boots, special socks, riding pants or flounced skirts, topped by yoked shirts trimmed with piping, accessorized with handkerchief scarves and narrow leather belts. You wouldn't want to rush out and buy it all, but you can take some direction as shown on page 10.

Attend Fashion Shows

Fashion shows are an easy way to see how outfits are put together. They also demonstrate how shapes look and move on the body. Make note of new fashion ideas — missing links that you want to add to your wardrobe. Recently, many stores have been featuring fashion shows highlighting larger sizes.

Observe the In-Store Displays

Often a store's display will tell a fashion story. For example, let's say a store might feature brightly colored tuck-in tops worn with slit skirts or fuller dirndl skirts. Jackets are fitted. Dresses are shown belted in softly knitted fabrics. What do these styles say to us? Well, we can take a hint. By sheer omission, we can see that in this example, pantsuits are out.

Go Snoop Shopping

Each season, retailers spend a fortune doing their fashion homework in the marketplaces of the world. A seasonal sampling of store windows can be a quick course in spotting important fashion silhouettes, colors, and fabrics.

Start your scrutinizing in the most expensive fashionable store in town. Looking is FREE, so screw up your courage and walk in like you are their best customer! Take mental note of store fashion displays. The object is to learn about color, texture, how combinations are put together. Train your eye to see line and scale. Scarf sizes. Print patterns. Handbag shapes. Pocket position. When you see the very best garments first, you'll learn to recognize good ready-to-wear copies in more reasonable price ranges. Or you can copy high-fashion originals by choosing a pattern and fabric and making the garment yourself. Try to absorb what you see. Later, you can jot down your impressions and file them.

Shop the Whole Store

Women's clothing is divided into so many categories. I suggest that you check out every department, paying special attention to mannequin displays.

In the beginning, don't try to apply any of what you see to yourself. This exercise is meant to stretch your imagination. Open up to the possibilities by wandering through all the fashion departments in the store. Feel at home in the Junior department, even if you have to pretend that you are shopping for a daughter. Soak up the fashion scenery. Make mental notes of styles you'd like to wear. In many cases, fashion trends begin in the Junior size range, but often they don't survive the test of translation into women's sizes. If you sew, you can see a style surfacing, and you can be the first one on your block to be wearing the latest thing!

Study In-Store Fashion Displays

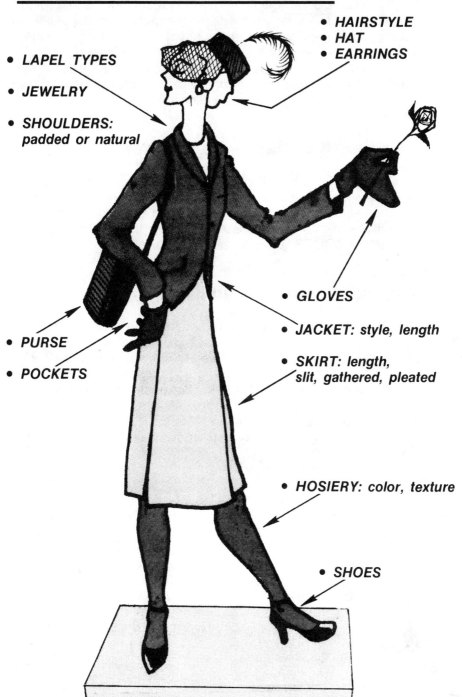

- **HAIRSTYLE**
- **HAT**
- **EARRINGS**

- **LAPEL TYPES**

- **JEWELRY**

- **SHOULDERS:**
  padded or natural

- **GLOVES**

- **JACKET:** style, length

- **SKIRT:** length,
  slit, gathered, pleated

- **PURSE**

- **POCKETS**

- **HOSIERY:** color, texture

- **SHOES**

Experiment With Your Clothes

Don't be discouraged by the extravagant clothes that seem to be created for those unreal skinny shapes. Instead, get a feel for the excitement, the drama, the effect that the clothes create. How are those emotions stirred? By colors? Flowing fabrics? Accessorization? You can learn to accomplish these same effects through experimenting with the clothes that you already have and by adding key new things.

Even the Men's Department

Ah! Don't overlook the Men's Department. A veritable gold mine! Notice the textures, fabrics, colors. They're a lot like women's clothes, aren't they? But often these garments are less expensive to buy, especially at sale time. And they are definitely LARGER. Do you see any correlation in styling?

Train Your Fashion Eye

By training your eye to differentiate between what's in and what's out, you are breaking down stored-up stereotypes of what you think you can wear. In addition, you need to look at a lot of clothes on many different figure types. "School" can be a spot on a bench at your local fashion mall. By repeating this process of separating the good from the bad, you are instinctively sharpening your shopping skills. Believe me, it won't take long to develop both good taste and a feeling for what styles look good on you.

To recap, commit today to begin your fashion education by:

- starting a fashion file
- reading fashion magazines and pattern company fashion information
- looking at fashion ads
- going shopping
- studying in-store and window displays
- trying on different styles in a store
- shopping fabric stores to see what kinds of yardage is available to duplicate ready-to-wear that's not available in your size or price range.
- attending fashion shows
- experimenting with accessorizing ideas at home

14

Does it all seem like a lot of work? Well, dressing fashionably does take extra effort. For those of us who have larger figures, we have to try even harder, but we can also have more fun rising to meet the challenge. All a smaller size needs to look sharp is money. Larger ladies need cash, plus a dose of fashionable enthusiasm. With a little concentrated effort, anyone can dress creatively, but it takes practice.

How much work it takes

CHAPTER THREE
Select Your Best Lines and Designs

McClue Studio. Kansas City

photo courtesy McCall's Patterns

No matter what size or shape our figure is in, there are certain optical tricks that fashion utilizes to create flattering styles. As you read this material, you need to keep in mind your personal dimensions and apply these rules so they work best for you.

Line

Line is the design element that carries the eye up or down, across or diagonally, as it' surveys the figure. Darts, tucks, seams all attract the eye. Fabrics with design or texture, such as stripes or ribs, also carry the eye in the direction that the design travels. Vertical lines are the most complimentary to fuller figures.

Horizontal lines can be worn anywhere when they are inconspicuous. For example, using a matching trim at the lower edge of a top would be better than a contrast trim.

Horizontal lines can be valuable if well-placed. If you have narrow shoulders, use horizontal lines to broaden them. If you have small legs, horizontal lines below the torso may be acceptable. Your mirror is your best friend. It will tell you if the lines are traveling in a flattering direction on your body.

Remember, accessories can also create favorable lines. Use accessories to add lengthening lines if a garment doesn't have them built in.

photo courtesy McCall's Patterns

McClue Studio, Kansas City

Even though top and bottom are soft contrast colors the scarf, necklace and tucks create flattering vertical lines.

Scale

The use of scale creates an element of balance that satisfies the eye. Scale has to do with how the size of things work together to create a complimentary overall effect. Just as an adult would look funny riding a pony, so does a single pearl seem out of place worn over an ample bosom.

So, the fuller figures can often successfully wear dramatic jewelry: try ropes of pearls, oversized medallions on long chains, large clumps of gold at the ear.

The secret is in selecting items that are of a compatible scale. For example, if you have a full figure, but delicate features (face, hands), you should avoid bulky jewelry. Select instead, a rope of pearls that will give you a long line for your silhouette, but in a smaller size.

The same goes for the scale of prints that a person can wear. Women who are tall can wear larger patterns than their shorter sister, no matter what size they are.

A tall large woman can wear large scale prints.

can use large light

or print that bump

photos courtesy McCall's Patterns
McClure Studio, Kansas City

A light, shiny blouse draws eye to face.

Color

Color is another important element of design. The eye travels to light and bright colors and to shiny surfaces first. Decide what part of your body you want people to look at first. Accent with a light color (ie. light blue, yellow or mint green) or use white. Try a bright color. Red is the most intense (brightest) of all colors.

Proportion

Another important element of design to be aware of is proportion. The ancient Greeks said the most interesting proportion to the eye is the 1/3-2/3 split. This applies to large or small women. A 50/50 split is not as pleasing. Also, using the lighter/brighter colors on top and darker/less intense on the bottom is more pleasing and will emphasize good proportion.

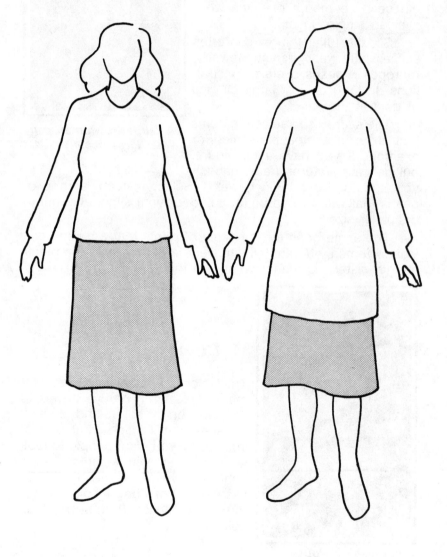

50/50 split   **1/3 - 2/3 split**

The same principle of proportion applies to tops and pants, especially when they are in two colors. A longer top will often be more pleasing and more interesting when worn with pants.

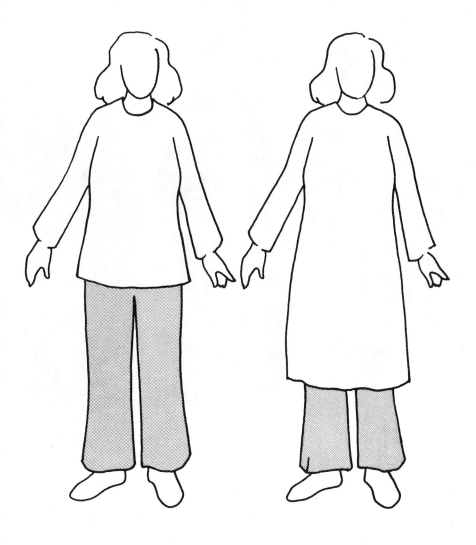

50/50 split   **2/3-1/3 split**

Color and Line Work Together to Create Illusion

Look how different this dress looks just by using color to change the emphasis of the lines. It could be a dress, or picture the same lines as a coat, jumper, or long vest over a dress. The overall effect is the same.

Where is your eye drawn first in each example?

Monochromatic Colors Camouflage Bad Lines

You can neutralize unflattering lines by using a monochromatic color scheme (one color or close shades of one color) for the entire outfit.

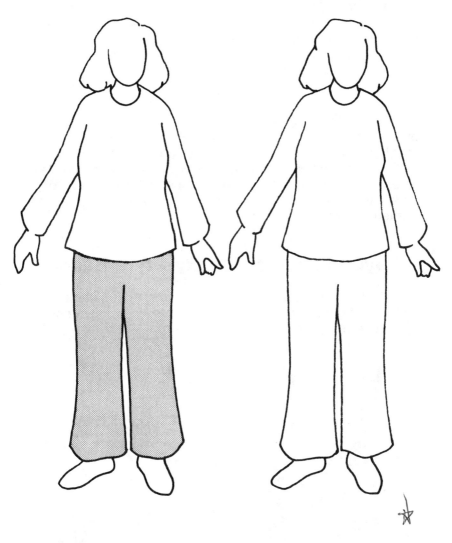

Two colors emphasize a less pleasing 50/50 split

Monochromatic colors make the split less noticeable

Layering Neutralizes Shapes

Layering is a tricky business. But the illusion that can be created using color combined in soft, lightweight fabrics makes it worthwhile to examine layering techniques.

I layer clothing year round, like a blouse under a tunic worn over a skirt or pants. Or a dress (fitted waistline) topped with either a blazer or an unbuttoned coatdress. In the summer I wear a sundress topped with a see-through tunic slit high to show the underdress.

In layering clothing, I choose voile, challis, jersey, polyester silkies, and crepes. If you want to top several thin layers off with a heavier fabric as I've done on page 25, that's o.k. But never put a heavy fabric on first, such as a bulky sweater under a jacket.

Color combinations are another reason to layer. Subtle colors in prints can be brought out when you add garments that highlight them. Also, elegant fashion color combinations can be created when more than one garment is worn such as camel mixed with burgundy. Camel for a suit. Burgundy for a blouse. Add burgundy as an easy shawl or a cape in jersey trimmed in camel.

Layering Increases My Style Range

Strapless and bare arm styles aren't the most flattering for most fuller figures, but you can use them successfully under a sheer coverup jacket or stole.

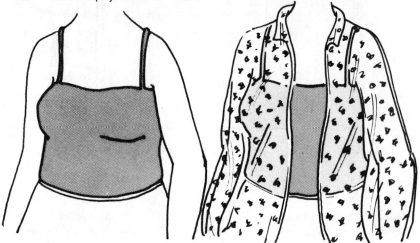

LAYERING in soft fabrics is the best trick I know for disguising figure faults.

Necklines Frame the Face

I think that the neckline of the dress/top that I wear is the most crucial part of the costume because that is what frames the neck and face. Always be aware of the neckline when looking at a dress or top.

If you have a short neck, for instance, you shouldn't choose a cowl or turtleneck style. Your neck will disappear, leaving your head awkwardly protruding from your shoulders! However, larger ladies with longer necks can wear these styles IF the fabric isn't too BULKY. Stay away from heavy knits and crocheted scarves that wrap around and around the neck.

On many larger figures one of the skinniest parts of the body is the collarbone area (upper chest). I wear my collars open in a "V" or choose a round or scoop neckline to accentuate the one area where my bones still show! For me, the test of whether a neckline is flattering is: Does it make my shape seem (1) longer/leaner, or (2) shorter/squatter? By all means, choose No. 1.

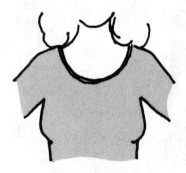

Round or Scoop — GOOD when circle is deep enough to frame shoulders and face. When used with gathers, center them in front and back keeping shoulders smooth for a more slimming effect.

Cowl or Draped — O.K., using jersey or light knits. The cowl effect is nice when used in the back, too. Full busted figures should avoid cowls with too much fullness across chest.

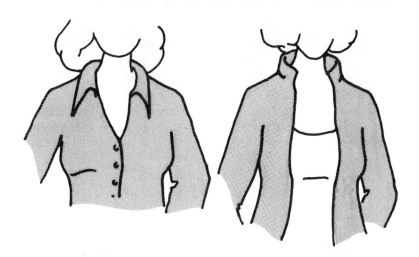

Open Collars — GOOD; the deeper V adds a lengthening look that flatters the face.

Mandarin — GOOD when worn as an open cardigan with a scoop neck T-shirt.

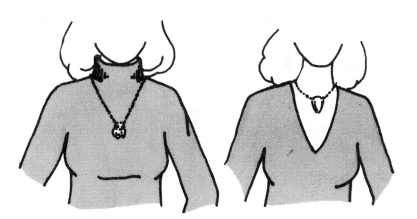

Turtleneck — GOOD when layered under a V-neck top. Short neck figures should avoid!

V-Neck — GOOD; can be softened by the addition of a scarf or jewelry. If you have a nice cleavage, one of the most attractive necklines for evening is a daring plunging "V".

Choose Easy to Wear Sleeves

I'm always looking for sleeve styles in pattern books and ready-to-wear that will camouflage my heavier upper arm and give me freedom of movement without broadening my silhouette. I look nice in set-in sleeves but I have to spend much more time fitting them. Most large figures have fuller upper arms like me, but if you're one of the fortunate few that doesn't — have fun with any style sleeve! These are some easy-to-fit, comfortable sleeve options.

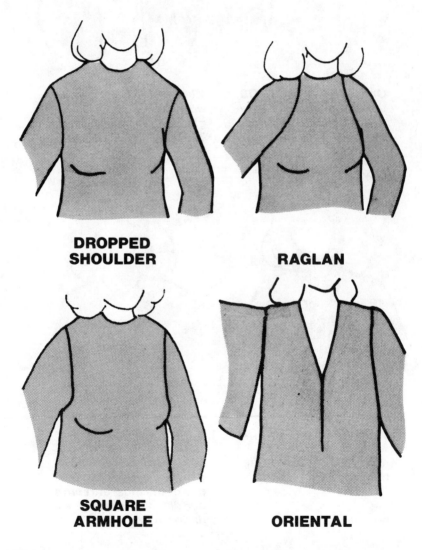

DROPPED SHOULDER

RAGLAN

SQUARE ARMHOLE

ORIENTAL

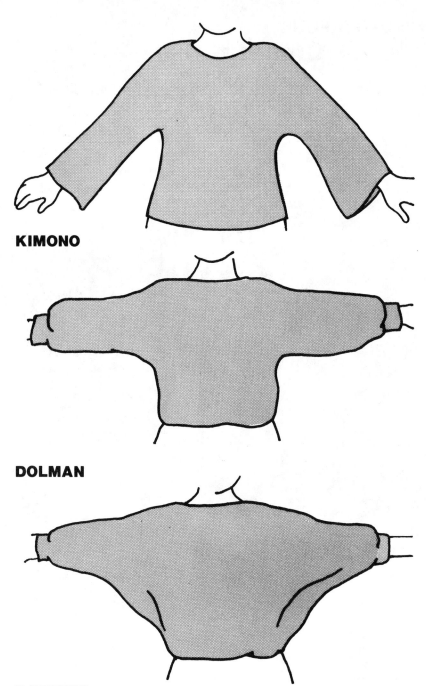

KIMONO

DOLMAN

BATWING

(This one is too bulky to wear under jackets!)

CHAPTER FOUR
Closet Closeup

*To toss
or not to toss,
THAT IS THE
QUESTION!!*

You're rarin' to go, right? You've got your fashion image firmly in mind and want to go shopping. HOLD IT! What about all the clothes in your closet? First, let's perform radical surgery on your existing wardrobe.

Diana Vreeland, longtime Vogue editor, reminds us that dressing fashionably is a habit; one that most of us need to improve.

My technique is to perform the CLOSET CLOSEUP ritual. The object is to sort out the saveables and to toss out the JUNK!

First, separate your wardrobe into two seasonal sections: Fall/Winter and Spring/Summer. (There may be some overlap). I suggest you keep your clothes organized in this manner with the current season up front. (I store my out-of-season clothing in a separate closet.)

Now, try on every garment in both piles. But before you start, comb your hair, put on your makeup and get out your jewelry, shoes, and other accessories and have them handy by your full-length mirror. Really, it's not fair to judge clothes out of context. Use your newly developed "fashion-vision" and remember, we're dressing the body that we're currently occupying; so don't try on your clothes with tomorrow in mind.

Rules for Tossing

There are some garments that just shouldn't be taking up space in your closet. Use the following rules for tossing:
1. If it absolutely doesn't fit . . . TOSS
2. It if is worn out . . . TOSS (if it only needs repair, do it NOW)
3. It if is a bad color . . . TOSS
4. If the style is unflattering . . . TOSS
5. If it's uncomfortable to wear . . . TOSS
6. If it doesn't make you feel great when you wear it (no matter how gorgeous or expensive it is) . . . TOSS

As you go, you may find a few garments that fit and look good, but seem "dull". Consider dyeing or remodeling them. I have cut a long dress in half, converting it into a two-piece street-length costume. Many "toss" garments may have salvagable parts!

Convert a Long Dress into Two Pieces

Many of us have floor-length caftans that can be quickly changed into clothing appropriate for daytime. Here is an illustration of one dress that I changed from long to short, just to give you an idea of what I mean.

I laid the gauze gown on the floor and placed a long top over it in order to decide length. I placed a skirt that was the correct length for me over the lower portion of the gown, matching the hems. The space that existed between the two garments became the hem for the top and the casing for the skirt.

I tried on the top before hemming, raising my arms and bending over to determine the exact length. I also tried on the skirt and decided to taper the waist in a little to get rid of some of the fullness. If the fabric had been less bulky, this would not have been necessary.

I finished the top by hemming the lower edge and the skirt by sewing a casing and threading elastic through it. The skirt was already hemmed . . . a hidden advantage!

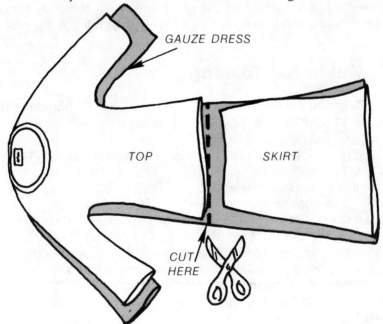

GAUZE DRESS

TOP

SKIRT

CUT HERE

I used lace that color-matched the dress, attaching it to the fabric edges of both the top and bottom, which caused it to hang nicely. I also trimmed the sleeves and neckline with the matching lace.

Update a Shirt That Fits

We all have utilitarian shirts in our wardrobe that are comfortable to wear, yet have a zero fashion rating. Adding trim or embroidery can give new life to old clothing. Try patchwork or applique, using up some of those golden oldies from your scraps. For inspiration and instruction, I use patterns, but some of you may be artistic enough to create your own masterpiece. Think of this newly transformed shirt as a lightweight jacket over a T-shirt and jeans, too.

embroidery added

Pick a Basic Color

Now you have a pile of "keepers." Divide the keepers into cool and warm weather piles. From these selections, you might be able to spot basic colors that you have a lot of or really like. If not, select a basic for winter and summer. It's good to select a basic wardrobe color from the neutrals: black, navy, brown, grey, burgundy, white, beige, or ivory. I use brown in the winter and ivory in the summer as basics to build upon. In selecting a basic color, remember that this is the color that most of your wardrobe should coordinate with, so be sure that if you choose pink you really like it and can live with it season after season. Usually, it's best to pick stronger colors as accents that can be tossed from time to time.

After you have separated your clothing into seasonal piles, you can take inventory. How many jackets, pants, blouses, sweaters, dresses, etc.?

No matter what authorities (including me) say, I don't think that there is any way to determine how many clothes and of what style a person should have in their wardrobe. Wardrobe size and type depends on the lifestyle that a person has . . . their job, their interests, their activities, how they entertain. Even though you are looking to me for advice, I <u>want</u> to <u>encourage you to experiment and find out what works</u> best for <u>you.</u> Dressing fashionably, <u>for me, means</u> dressing CREA-TIVELY, which eliminates the absolutes!

So now you know if there is a color in your closet that you like and whether you have a lot of clothes made out of it. And you know how many of everything you own. You should also make an effort to see how your wardrobe works together.

Play With Your Clothes Before Adding Anything

Play dress-up again, but this time consider the clothing building blocks that can be interchanged. Your fashion homework will stand you in good stead now. Use all of your accumulated knowledge to coordinate some new combinations of your old clothing. Put together pants, shirts, and sweaters in coordinated units. Are you missing a crucial unit? Could you add one skirt and create several new outfits? Would a velvet blazer open up a new way to wear several other older garments? Each season, it's fun to play this game. You'll be surprised how good you get at making new combinations. The trick is to forget how you have been wearing your things and start from scratch.

The dream wardrobe always has "ITEMS." ITEMS, as I call them, are your extras that add just the right touch to your outfit. A special sweater. A scarf or shawl. A unique piece of jewelry. A crocheted tunic. A velvet vest. ITEMS are the stuff individuality is made of. For more about ITEMS, see Chapter 12.

Make a Want List, Strive for Balance

Knowing what we have gives us some idea of what we need. We are striving for balance. If an inventory shows a glut of pantsuits, then dresses and skirts are essential. If there is a record of all neutral colors with few fashion colors, then shop for colors in fabrics that add variety.

What are the areas that you aren't geared up for? How about entertaining or going out? Do you have clothing appropriate for active sports? You'd probably do more of both if you did. With our information at hand, we can now make a list of what we should make and what we should buy.

As I look in my closet, I see too many clothes, because collecting clothes is my hobby. I have a lot of clothes besides my basics in varying color groupings. But I started small with just the clothes that I needed, and you should do the same. Shop according to your economic condition, your sewing skills, and your shopping experience.

Fashion Mixes Old with New

Your "want" list might be enormous at this point. You might want to upgrade your sewing skills, so that you can make more of your clothing. But I caution you on one point: Don't try to sew your whole wardrobe. Remember the word BALANCE. A fashionable wardrobe is a mixture of new, old, ready-to-wear and handsewn clothing. (Even we home economists don't attempt to sew it all!) And we might need to add some jazzy accessories to spark up our older outfits.

It may take you several seasons to put your fashion wardrobe into working order. But our CLOSET CLOSEUP has given us some practical insight into where to begin to build.

Also, it demonstrates that size isn't the stumbling block to better dressing that we thought it to be. The question really is, can you turn your wardrobe into a fashion reservoir that you can draw from for every occasion? It takes planning and organization, putting clothes into a correct perspective.

CHAPTER FIVE

Why Shop for Ready-to-wear?

"Have I over-done the Western bit?"

It's nearly impossible to try to sew everything and there are also times when you find something terrific, ready-made, that you couldn't afford to make. I call those "finds". Plus, I would never dream of beginning a seasonal sewing session without first checking out the retail market place. Why? I can avoid costly mistakes in picking the wrong style pattern, color or fabric.

At the store:

● I can try on ready-to-wear to see how NEW silhouettes work for my shape . . . jacket lengths, skirt lengths, blouses tucked in or out . . . do tunics work?

● I can see the latest fabrics and see how they feel on my body. I can even try on EXPENSIVE silks and synthetic suedes. Are fabrics or textures too bulky, slinky, dull or busy? Those 3-way mirrors can be very honest.

● Color — I can decide if I feel good in head-to-toe cerise, or if I'd better settle for a touch at the neck. (Too bad the lighting in some dressing rooms isn't better).

● Best of all, because new fashions are in stores very early in the season, I can use the time to plan my wardrobe ahead and have time for sewing projects.

Other Shopping Pluses

Usually, I don't go shopping for ready-to-wear with a commitment to buy, because I am a bargain shopper. I think that everyone should be open to saving money. A good buy for me is finding a quality garment that is priced below what it would cost me to make it for myself . . . or finding a garment that exceeds my ability to sew it for a price that I can afford. In both cases, when I find it, if it fits well, I buy it. Fashion that fits is always a bargain!

Another advantage of buying well-priced ready-made garments is obvious. The time and money saved can be converted into making special handsewn clothing.

The question is "how can we avoid accumulating clothing on sale that looks dated after one season?". When the Big Top phased out, I purchased several at bargain prices (in beautiful fabrics!). My big tops were classic shirt styles, so even on sale, I wasn't making an impulsive purchase. When closer to the body styling came into fashion, I slimmed down the tops by tapering the underarm seams.

Key to Sew or Buy (handwritten margin note)

Shop the Sales

Often RTW dresses are good buys if they contain large quantities of expensive fabric, and have flattering lines. For example, I bought a batwing sleeve wool jersey dress (see opposite page) for $15. I wear it belted and blousoned. With dramatic jewelry the effect is both fashionable and flattering, as well as being a boost to my clothing budget!

It takes practice to successfully buy ready-to-wear that's useable on sale. Sometimes it means buying off-season. (However, even totally frivolous purchases that have a short fashion life can be rationalized if the price is right).

Not everything needs to be on sale. If you find a perfect garment, buy it no matter what the price. The larger customer still doesn't have that many choices.

Check Every Department

When we are shopping, it's important to realize that clothes are just clothes. I shop everywhere, including maternity, since I don't consider my size to be a limitation, but rather my immediate condition. All methods that I am recommending I have always practiced and always will, slim or stout. Forget about "stigma". Remember, you're shopping for ideas and inspiration. They are free for the looking.

Key to large ladies

For my figure, a soft flowing unfitted dress in a basic color is a good investment, whether hand sewn or ready-made.
When a more fitted silhouette comes into play, I simply add a tie belt and wear the dress in a blouson style.

Shop Menswear

Remember, I mentioned earlier to check out the menswear department for trends. I also want to encourage you to look for clothing for yourself there. I do. Sweaters, shirts, warmups, shorts. Sometimes I find fashions that fit for bargain prices compared to what I would pay in the women's department across the aisle.

No one can tell the difference between men's and women's warmup outfits. The same goes for pullover sweaters and pull-on pants with drawstring waists. I'm really not as cheap as I sound. It's just that after years of trying on so many too-small items in the women's department, I find pleasure in taking my business elsewhere!

There are some fit problems to make note of, when shopping in men's stores. Men's pants often have skinny legs, so I always buy an extra-large size, even when it means taking in the waist a bit. However, I usually buy drawstring-waist pants, so it doesn't matter.

I do buy men's shirts (large size), even though the buttons are on the "wrong side", because I don't think that when the shirt is on me anyone can tell the difference. Sometimes I have to shorten the sleeves or vent the side seams for tummy ease.

In the beginning, I pretended that I was shopping for the two men in our family, to sort of justify my presence in the men's department. But now I just walk in. You may want to order menswear from a catalog to see how things fit you. I'll have to admit, I've never gone to a fitting room to try things on! As more and more large-size ready-to-wear emerges, I may phase out menswear shopping. So far, I still find fashions I like at a good price.

Look for Quality

Another important consideration in buying ready-to-wear is the built-in quality of a garment. It's a fact that fuller figures quickly damage poorly constructed garments. Often, it is a wise investment to pay more for a fully lined garment that has been carefully tailored. If you don't have tailoring skills, your money is well spent on quality ready-made tailored clothing.

A case in point is the Pendleton Woolen Mills women's ready-to-wear clothing line. This company was among the first to offer large-size better woolen clothing on the market. Their styles are classic, and the quality and construction is impeccable. If you wear wool, I consider these garments a good investment, although I hesitate to mention brands, since in most cases manufacturers aren't consistent in what they offer from season to season. Another plus for Pendleton. Each season, you can purchase their coordinating woolen yardage in 60-inch widths that will allow you to make a multitude of coordinates to wear with your purchased garments.

Ask Your Retailer for Help

Watch for more and more better large-size merchandise. Designers such as Gloria Vanderbilt and Pierre Cardin are only the forerunners of a long list who supply fuller-figure apparel.

If you can't find what you want, I encourage you to make your wishes known to your local clothing retailers. Their buyers will respond, offering you a better shopping selection. I know that quality fashion merchandise is available to these stores since I see it advertised in retail trade papers.

Use Catalogs

Also, I should mention that for years I have used catalogs to buy large-sized clothing, especially jeans. I feel catalogs (Sears, J.C. Penney, Wards) offer good-quality merchandise at reasonable prices. Their sizing seems a bit skimpy, so I usually buy a size larger. I find catalogs are a good place to shop for underwear, too. However, many retail stores are increasing their larger-size stock, so check there first, since it is handier to be able to see the merchandise and try it on.

I also rely on mail order catalogs for fashion inspiration and subscribe to as many as I can. I learn so much about accessorization and new uses of color and textures from them.

Carry Swatches

One of the worst temptations, for me, is impulse buying. It helps to carry representative fabric swatches along that will assist you in selecting clothing that complements and coordinates with your wardrobe. One method is to put these fabric swatches into the plastic window pouches that fit into a wallet. They can easily be pulled out and used for comparison. In a sense, it's like carrying your whole wardrobe in your purse.

What Size Ready-to-wear To Buy

Shopping for size is a real challenge. Sometimes manufacturers seem to change fit from season to season which of course is because of styling change. I always try clothes on to be assured of good fit.

When close-to-body is fashion's feeling, the only ready-to-wear we can buy without altering is available in the custom size department.

The biggest single difficulty I've discovered in buying fitted large-size ready-to-wear is that the collar/neckline is too large when I purchase a garment that fits me everywhere else. You can see this in large-size clothing ads . . . the neck fit is pitiful! An advantage of sewing is that you can buy the pattern to fit your neck — that is, the shoulder/bust area and add to the tummy and hip area until it fits.

A classic case of "gaposis of the collar."

Remember that in a loose-fitting garment, a person can often wear a much smaller size (11-14), thus solving the shoulder/neckline fit problems. But check the sleeve fit as you may need to avoid styles with tight, set-in-sleeves when using a smaller size.

I sound like all large figures are smaller on the top than on the bottom. You may be the exception, but on the whole, I think I'm right. It seems to be common no matter what size a person is. Perhaps it is because we are a "sit-down" society.

Price Affects Size

The price of the garment often affects the sizing. The rule of thumb being the cheaper the price the larger the size you wear, and vice versa. In RTW that is called "Vanity Sizing". Spending money is only painless when we buy wisely. I encourage you to become an "educated" shopper.

CHAPTER SIX
Shopping for Fabric

Stiff fabrics make me look like a knight in heavy armor.

For me, the feeling of fashion starts with fabric. If I were a designer, I'd live in fabric libraries. I sew because I fall in love with a piece of fabric, or I see some garment in the store that I can't afford, but the fabric is so great that I want to copy it. I feel that there is an instant chemistry that is created when the right style is combined with the perfect fabric. You know you are going to look great and feel fabulous, even when the garment is still in yardage and pattern pieces. Although we need basics, fashion is the salt in our stew and fabric is the meat of it.

Choose Fabrics You Love

There is no rule of thumb for fabric selection. It's a matter of personal taste, taking into consideration the directions that fashion takes each season. The choice between wovens and knits and colors and textures are dictated to a point, and the fashion student needs to stay current.

Personally, I choose softer fabrics, usually, because I like to layer several garments. Also, I like the drapey look that soft fabrics give me. I often choose:

voile	velour	crepe	chambray
challis	knitted suede	lace	jersey
velvet	cotton interlock	gauze	terrycloth

I avoid most 100% polyesters because I find the fabrics don't allow for proper air circulation between my skin and garment, making me too hot. 100% natural fibers, or natural fibers blended with synthetics, are my favorites because they allow more breathability.

A fabric's hand or feel often wins me over, but again there are no rules. Take into consideration the use of the garment. For pants, I would use a much more durable fabric than I would for a loose fitting dress.

One fiber that we are hearing more about today is rayon. I mention it because rayon challis is one of my favorites. Challis is a gem to wear because it is cool for its weight and drapes wonderfully. Rayon, when blended with synthetics makes fabrics that are washable and are relatively wrinkle free.

Nothing can be absolute today, with the fabric market changing so quickly and prices climbing so steadily. Gone forever are the 99-cents-a-yard polyester knits (and I say, hooray!). Too many of us got trapped in our pink and yellow pantsuits and forgot to move on to more fashionable looks.

Natural fibers are gaining popularity, but in many cases they are the most costly. There's nothing wrong with buying an "imitation." Silk-like polyesters are the best example of man improving upon nature. Silk is a fabulous fiber, but it takes considerable care in sewing and maintenance. Silky polyesters have a look and hand that is so close to the real thing that you can fool the experts, and the price is reasonable. I have a few silk garments, but for everyday, I use "imitations."

Larger figures can wear almost all fabrics — firmer fabrics for tailored looks like my blazer and skirt, softer, more drapable fabrics for my flowing caftan.

Choose Fabric for YOUR Body

Stand before a full-length mirror and drape the fabric over your shoulder to see how it is going to look BEFORE you buy. Do the color, texture or pattern look good on you? How does the fabric drape or hang on your body? I duplicate the style I want to make while draping, such as a V-neckline dress with a blouson waist, to see what the finished garment would look like.

Buy Enough Fabric

Regarding how much fabric to buy in contrast to the amount suggested on the pattern envelope:

The yardage suggestions made by the pattern companies are now very accurate, thanks to computerization. So, if you are like me and buy patterns sized to fit your shoulders and neckline, be sure to buy extra yardage to accommodate the extra inches you'll need to add (using Thelen's Law, pages 75 & 76) to fit your torso. I also add several inches at the bottom of my pattern pieces to allow me to change the waistline for blousoning, etc. (However, remember that I'm 5'8"). Sometimes, you'll need an additional ¼ to ½ yard depending on layout and fabric width.

Another way to lay out a pattern when you don't have enough fabric is to use the crossgrain and take advantage of the fabric width. However, I have learned the hard way that this type of frugality sometimes creates unhappy results, as crossgrain hangs differently. Be sure to test the drapability of a crossgrain fabric by holding the material up and draping it over your shoulder.

If you are buying expensive fabric, don't hesitate to ask to lay out the pattern on the yardage in the store to get an accurate estimate of how much you need to buy. Or you can make up the pattern in a cheap fabric like I did before buying $50 a yard Italian silk. In that way, I solved two dilemmas. I learned if the design really looked good enough to invest all that time and money in, and I knew exactly how much material I needed to buy.

Include Unusual Fabrics

I like special fabrics like batik, chintz, eyelet and lace. Linen or linen look-alikes are great for tailored looks, but experiment with the weight that works for you. I avoid stiff, boardy fabrics like the plague, because they are uncomfortable to wear and add too much bulk.

Each season, new versions of popular fabrics come out, often in differing weights. Even synthetic suede fabrics are now coming in lighter weights.

My Love Affair with Lace

Lace is my all-time favorite accessory fabric. I make a lot of ITEMS from lace because it creates such a dramatic illusion. People aren't used to seeing it except on evening wear and lingerie. I wear lace with Levis®. The cover photo shows me wearing a lace top over a black lounging outfit. My bathing suit coverup is lace.

My favorite "Item" is a lace coverup over sleeveless garments like this tube-top sundress.

A lace vest adds interest to my Levis®

I must admit that much of my inspiration and lace fabric comes from my friend Jessica McClintock, owner/designer of Gunne Sax, a California dress manufacturer. Jessica is the largest user of lace yardage in the U.S. When I visit her design rooms, see her clothes, feel her fabrics, I come away so inspired to make magical clothes. (Sometimes I luck out, when she makes a one-size-fits-all creation, and come home with a ready-to-wear masterpiece.) Again, you will have to find what fabrics can work "magic" for you. But don't be shy about trying "glamour" fabrics out as "ITEMS." Accessories are meant to be traffic stoppers. You'll be amazed how a simple jacket pattern can be translated into a *piece de resistance* when done in a fabulous fabric. Chapter 12 will give you more ideas.

Make a Mini-Wardrobe

As a method of experimenting with new fabrics and color, each season I make a "Mini-Wardrobe". This grouping is my "High Fashion" sewing project. Sometimes, I choose designs that are "far out", sometimes classic, depending on fashion trends.

In the case of the black linen suit (seen pictured), it was experimental in that I hadn't worn a tucked-in blouse with a straight skirt in years. Black and white were strongly featured colors that season, so I went with them, adding color with print fabrics and accessories. It was nice to use black linen, in that the suit could be worn year-round, but that wasn't my motivation. If the season's top-priority color had been RED, I would have found a shade of red that I could have lived with!

I chose linen (actually a polyester/linen blend) because the fabric tailored nicely and had enough body to fit and not bag as might a more loosely woven fabric. Also the linen was firm enough that it didn't require a lining for stabilizing or finishing, so it made cooler, easy-to-wear garments.

I discovered the challis for the skirt among my stored fabrics. The softness of the fabric complimented the tri-color print. I chose a skirt pattern that was cut on the bias for maximum movability. It's important to remember to periodically recheck your fabric stash for both inspiration and as an economy measure.

My "Mini Wardrobe" — I made the black suit and print challis skirt to coordinate. I bought the T-shirt and bolero — a nice balance of handsewn and ready-made garments.

Remnants and Sales

A word about remnants. Don't overlook them. Often you can find a yard of expensive panne velvet that would make a great bolero to top off last season's dinner dress. Or a quarter-yard of silk that could be the perfect suit scarf.

It's important to remember that you can't always buy the right remnant at the time that you want to use it. So you have to tune in and buy good fabrics when you see them on sale. The secret is not to pay too much and to limit yourself to fabrics that you wouldn't ordinarily purchase in advance of usage.

Avoid buying strong prints or colors in volume. Our larger silhouettes are easily "overexposed". Unless there is a special effect that you are trying to create, I find it best to keep "brights" to a minimum. That doesn't mean always wear black. But I do recommend moderation when it comes to wearing hot pink top to bottom. Remnants are a great resource for that added color accent some fashion outfits need.

One suggestion for proper use of stored remnants and fabrics is to have a fiber file. One method would be to clip a corner of each piece of stored yardage and attach it to a 3x5 card, listing the yardage amount. Before fabric shopping, recheck this file. We all have little gems stashed away that we tend to forget about that can be used up in this manner.

Moderation is the Key to Success

I once heard about a 200-pound woman who loved hot pink but never wore it because she felt it made her look more than her ample size. One day she suddenly realized, "Hey! I do weigh 200 pounds and I do LOVE hot pink." Excitedly, she went right out and bought a wonderful hot pink fabric and made up a dress that she loved. I thought that it was neat that she overcame her fear of what other people might think and started pleasing herself. Sometimes what makes you feel good can add such a glow about you, that you look great — even if it's not your best color or line.

Moderation is what works best, on the average. Avoid heavy textures all over. The same goes for prints. They make a person's shape look bulky. I like paisleys or watercolor abstracts. I love prints on sheer fabrics, because they sort of blend from a distance.

By all means, try to steer clear of overkill. If you want a glitter effect, choose a fabric with a Lurex® thread woven through it that adds sparkle. A shiny shawl would be nice. But wall-to-wall sequins would be too much. Why be a moving target?

Upgrade!

I just can't say enough about fabric. Again, practice will give you confidence to start buying more expensive yardage. I've been sewing off and on for ten years, and it still scares me to cut into $14-a-yard cotton batik, but the results are worth it. I wouldn't take a million dollars for my BIG BLUE BOXCAR COAT (see page 57).

You see, sometimes fashion just demands that we spend money on a fashion fabric. You can't get a "mohair" look from wool flannel. Either you go for it, or you settle for second best. I want you to have courage and commitment to make beautiful clothing. Everyone, regardless of size, should experience the finer things in life! I think that beautiful clothing helps us recognize our own beauty as human beings. It may be just a game, but we all want to feel like winners, don't we?

CHAPTER SEVEN
Measuring Up

Now we know how we want to look, so it's time to translate our dreams into reality. But before plunging ahead, we need to take a few further "measures".

The importance of completing this "Truth in Packaging" inventory is to get the facts and be ready to dress the body shape that you are today. You may be surprised by what the tape tells you about your body. Sometimes, our eyes trick us by refusing to see certain changes in our figures. That's our mind again, comparing . . . remembering when we were this or that shape. Our new plan is based on fitting the figure that we currently have and becoming skilled enough to make any changes necessary to accommodate for inches that come and go.

We will use these "actuals" to determine optimum blouse, jacket, skirt and dress measurements. Then we can choose flattering styles, because we'll know about the shape that we need to "cover".

It's been my experience that it's hard to get from A to B without a map, especially when I haven't made the trip before. By recording our measurement, we are taking the second step in creating our new fashion image.

Ask anyone . . . what is the true measure of fine fashion? Always, the look based on FIT . . . never size. This may be the hardest work you'll have to do . . . facing up to FIT.

For those of you who are precise by inclinati mechanics of measuring will be a breeze for you. In fac probably have an up-to-date chart at your fingertips. The lowing information and encouragement is for those of us wh find the tape measure too truthful and the process too tedious; so we've never gone the whole way.

I feel that this step is essential. I've discovered that as my figure expanded, I continued to visualize myself several sizes smaller than I actually was by focusing on my face, hands, feet, etc., while ignoring my larger middle. That's okay when you're buying lipstick and shoes, but it raises havoc when you have to buy a pair of jeans. I found that manning my trusty tape measure and confronting myself in the full-length mirror gave me the stimulus to create a wardrobe that flatters the figure that I currently occupy!

Underthings are Important

But before manning our tapes, it's necessary to ask, "Are you wearing a well-fitted bra?" Because if you aren't, I can guarantee that none of your clothes will fit properly or look attractive no matter how "fashionable" the design. A sagging bustline ages any figure. And let's face it: most of us need support.

Women who have grown up "big busted" have long ago invested in a well-fitted bra. But many of us have added inches "around" and are trying to get by using bra extenders on worn-out bras.

I can recommend looking under "brassieres" in the Yellow Pages of your phone book, if you live in a metropolitan area. There are usually several specialty shops listed that have persons specially trained to fit larger figures. For those who live in rural areas, large mail-order catalogs offer large-size merchandise (Wards, J.C. Penney, Sears). Strangely, this stock isn't always available in their retail stores.

To assure our successful transformation from the "ugly duckling" into the "beautiful swan", we needed to start from the inside and work out. First, we learned how to change our attitude. Then, how to upgrade our underwear. If you need to, go shopping NOW.

The next step is to find a friend you can trust, because we'll need their help in recording the "bare" facts. You see, proper fit requires correct use of the tape measure, and there can measure themselves. It may be traumatic, ...etting-to-know-ourselves program deals with ...XACTLY what our figure looks like.

...e It Exam

...friend arrives, take the "LET'S FACE IT" ...XAM. To pass it, you must take off all of your clothes and stand in front of a full-length mirror. Edith Head, fashion designer, suggests that this be done while wearing a brown paper bag with eyeholes over one's head to eliminate the possibility of concentrating on the familiar face, while ignoring a less familiar body. SCRUTINIZE.

- Where am I fat?
- Where am I thin?
- Do I have any lumps or bumps?
- Is one side high or low?
- Do my shoulders slope?
- Where are my best features . . . long legs, slender ankles?
- Where do I need camouflage?

This eyeballing exercise is necessary. It teaches us two lessons: 1) what shape our body is actually in, *without help.* 2) how we see ourselves . . . *without clothes, fantasy goes!*

Now the measuring tape workout. The following charts may seem overly elaborate, especially when most of us make unfitted garments, but somewhere along the line you'll need these measurements. The diagrams will assist you in tape placement. Be accurate. Cheating now won't change your body size later, when you put on your finished garment. Don't hold your breath, suck in your stomach or contract your hips, unless you intend to remain in that posture permanently. For this exercise wear your new bra and panties.

After you have taken your measurements, you can check them against pattern measurement charts and ready-to-wear catalog charts (see samples on page 65) to ascertain your correct size. You may discover that you are between sizes or a half-size. If you fall between the cracks on sizing, it usually works to buy the smaller-sized pattern, but in ready-to-wear, I usually buy the larger-sized garment. You can add inches where you need them when you are cutting out a pattern, but you can't add inches around to a pair of ready-made pants that are too tight!

The paper bag trick . . .
WITHOUT CLOTHES,
FANTASY
GOES!

Measuring Tips:

1. a. BUST — Tape over fullest part. Be careful not to let tape slip down the back.
    b. HIGH BUST — Raise tape 3-5 inches above full bust and keep tape at same place in back.

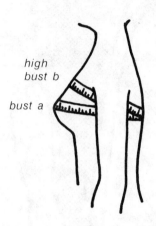

2. WAIST — Tie ¼" wide elastic around waist to establish natural waist line and measure around at the elastic.
3. HIPS
    a. High Hip . . . 3-4 inches below waist
    b. Low Hip . . . 7-8 inches below waist (or fullest part)
    c. Thighs . . . locate the widest point. Measure.
4. BACK WAIST LENGTH — Measure from nape of neck to center back of natural waistline.
5. FRONT WAIST LENGTH — Measure over bust from shoulder to waist.
6. NECK — Measure around base of neck.
7. SHOULDER WIDTH — Measure from side of neck to shoulder bone.
8. BACK WIDTH — Measure back from underarm to underarm 9" below neck.
9. ARMHOLE DEPTH
    a. Back — measure from shoulder bone to under arm
    b. Front — measure from shoulder bone to under arm

10. ARMS
    a. Fullest part of upper arm - with elbow bent
    b. Wrist
    c. With arm bent (hand on hip) measure from shoulder to elbow to wrist
11. LEG
    a. Around fullest part of thigh (one leg)
    b. Around knee
    c. Around calf
    d. From waistline to floor
    e. From crotch to floor
12. CROTCH DEPTH — Outside leg measurement (11d) minus inside leg measurement (11e).

LENGTH OF SKIRTS, DRESSES AND PANTS — I suggest that you take the length from an existing garment that looks good on you or put in the hem when the garment that you are sewing is finished. If you are extra tall, allow several extra inches when cutting out your patterns.

Date your chart. Re-measuring is only necessary with extreme weight loss or gain; however, every six months you might recheck to see if you've shifted.

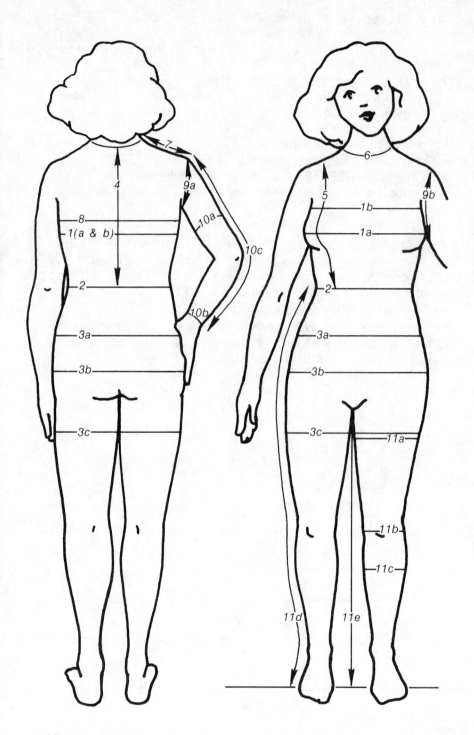

Measurement Chart

	ME	+ EASE* =	TOTAL
1. a. BUST		2-3 "	
b. HIGH BUST			
2. WAIST		1 "	
3. a. HIGH HIP			
b. LOW HIP		2 "	
c. THIGHS			
4. BACK WAIST LENGTH		¼"	
5. FRONT WAIST LENGTH		¼"	
6. NECK			
7. SHOULDER WIDTH			
8. BACK WIDTH		½-1 "	
9. a. BACK ARMHOLE DEPTH			
b. FRONT ARMHOLE DEPTH			
10. a. UPPER ARM		2½"	
b. WRIST			
c. ARM LENGTH			
11. a. THIGH			
b. KNEE			
c. CALF			
d. OUTSIDE LENGTH			
e. INSIDE LENGTH			
12. CROTCH DEPTH (11d minus 11e)		¾-1¼"	

*minimum ease — a pattern should be cut larger by these minimum amounts for comfort unless you are using a very stretchy knit. (see page 72.)

CHAPTER EIGHT

How to Buy Patterns

description

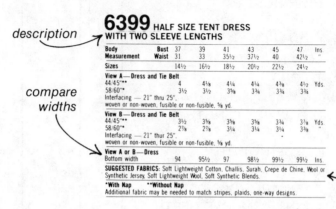

6399 HALF SIZE TENT DRESS
WITH TWO SLEEVE LENGTHS

compare widths

Body								
Body Measurement	**Bust**	37	39	41	43	45	47	Ins.
	Waist	31	33	35½	37½	40	42½	"
Sizes			14½	16½	18½	20½	22½	24½	

View A—Dress and Tie Belt

44/45"**	4	4⅛	4¼	4¼	4⅜	4½	Yds.
58/60"*	3½	3½	3⅝	3¾	3¾	3¾	
Interfacing — 21" thru 25", woven or non-woven, fusible or non-fusible, ⅝ yd.							

View B—Dress and Tie Belt

44/45"**	3½	3⅝	3⅝	3⅝	3¾	3⅞	Yds.
58/60"*	2⅞	2⅞	3¼	3¼	3¼	3⅜	"
Interfacing — 21" thur 25", woven or non-woven, fusible or non-fusible, ⅝ yd.							

View A or B—Dress

Bottom width	94	95½	97	98½	99½	99½	Ins.

SUGGESTED FABRICS: Soft Lightweight Cotton, Challis, Surah, Crepe de Chine, Wool or Synthetic Jersey, Soft Lightweight Wool, Soft Synthetic Blends.

*With Nap   **Without Nap
Additional fabric may be needed to match stripes, plaids, one-way designs.

fabric suggestion

line art for exact fitting lines and shape

Art: courtesy McCalls Patterns

Helpful hints found in your pattern book.

Here are some ideas that you may find helpful when you go shopping for patterns:

1. Look carefully at the line drawings. They are clear illustrations of the true lines in that garment. How to adapt those lines to your body is your choice.

2. Read the entire pattern book. Remember, you might be small enough on top to use the Misses size range as long as you enlarge the bottom. Take a look at the large size sections each month as the pattern companies are making many changes you'll love. As you did in ready-to-wear, shop the men's and maternity sections.

3. Stay simple. I strive to keep all the garments that I sew simple for several good reasons: Number 1 is that I hate to rip out and, using my "creative" techniques, "fancy" often translates into "failure"! Also my fuller figure is flattered by simple, flowing lines or trim, neatly tailored styles. My advice to anyone other than advanced, skilled seamstresses is to stay simple and SMILE.

4. If you see a pattern that you like in your size, don't let the season pass without buying it. They are frequently discontinued. I consider my pattern library an important part of my fashion reservoir. I can draw upon its vast potential anytime a piece of fabric attracts my attention, or when a surprise event comes up that calls for something quick and new.

5. As you go through the pattern book, look for ITEMS that can add spice to your wardrobe. I've made overskirts from apron patterns, evening dresses from lingerie patterns, and bathrobes from bathing suit cover-ups.

6. Check the additional pages in the beginning of the pattern book for fashion trends.

7. Never assume that the colors or fabrics used by the pattern company in a photo or illustration are the only choices you have.

Buy the Correct Pattern Size

We can easily agree, based on our experience, that rarely does a person gain weight in equal dimensions over her entire body. Most of us have gotten thicker in the middle, upper arm and thighs. I formulated "THELEN'S LAW" to explain how to solve this dilemma. On pages 75 & 76 THELEN'S LAW is described in detail, but basically I recommend that we buy patterns that fit our shoulders and neckline, using the bust and/or high bust measurement to ascertain pattern size. We'll add inches below to fit the rest of our body when the time comes to cut and sew.

You may have been purchasing patterns that were too large, if your hips or bust are larger in proportion to the rest of your figure. When we sew with a too-large pattern, we compound our sewing difficulties.

Follow these Steps for Better Fit:

1. First, record accurate body measurements (page 61).
2. Compare your measurements to the charts in the pattern book.
3. If you fall between sizes, buy the smaller size (the standard ease built into all patterns protects you).
4. Buy *tops and dresses* using your bust measurement and simply add extra fabric to the body where needed.

   EXCEPTION: If your bust measures 2½ inches or more larger than your high bust (see page 58), substitute your high bust measurement for bust when buying pattern. The reason for this is that patterns are graded for a "B" bra cup and fuller busted figures measure out of proportion to what the rest of the body needs for proper fit. It's smart to buy a pattern that fits correctly in the high bust area and alter for a full bust (see page 77).

5. Buy *full skirts* by waist size.
6. Buy *straight skirts and pants* by hip size.
7. Buy *coordinates* to fit your top, and apply THELEN'S LAW to the rest.

MISSES'

Misses' patterns are designed for a well proportioned, and developed figure; about 5'5" to 5'6" without shoes.

Size	6	8	10	12	14	16	18	20	22	24
Bust	30½	31½	32½	34	36	38	40	42	44	46
Waist	23	24	25	26½	28	30	32	34	37	39
Hip	32½	33½	34½	36	38	40	42	44	46	48
Back Waist Length	15½	15¾	16	16¼	16½	16¾	17	17¼	17⅜	17½

Sample charts from McCall's Pattern Book (All pattern company charts are standard.)

HALF-SIZE

Half-size patterns are for a fully developed figure with a short backwaist length. Waist and hip are larger in proportion to bust than other figure types; about 5'2" to 5'3" without shoes.

Size	10½	12½	14½	16½	18½	20½	22½	24½
Bust	33	35	37	39	41	43	45	47
Waist	27	29	31	33	35	37½	40	42½
Hip	35	37	39	41	43	45½	48	50½
Back Waist Length	15	15¼	15½	15¾	15⅞	16	16⅛	16¼

WOMEN'S

Women's patterns are designed for the larger, more fully mature figure; about 5'5" to 5'6" without shoes.

Size	38	40	42	44	46	48	50
Bust	42	44	46	48	50	52	54
Waist	35	37	39	41½	44	46½	49
Hip	44	46	48	50	52	54	56
Back Waist Length	17¼	17⅜	17½	17⅝	17¾	17⅞	18

Sample charts from Montgomery Ward Catalog.

Women's dress sizes: 38–44

Order size	38	40	42	44
If bust measures	41-42½	43-44½	45-46½	47-48½
If waist measures	35-36½	37-38½	39-41	41½-43½
If hips measure	42-43½	44-45½	46-47½	48-49½

Misses sizes:

Order size	16	18	20	22
If bust measures	37½-38½	39-40½	41-42½	43-44½
If waist measures	29½-30½	31-32½	33-34½	35-36½
If hips measure	40-41	41½-43	43½-45	45½-47

Half Size Chart: 14½ thru 26½

Order size	14½	16½	18½	20½	22½	24½
If bust measures	37-38½	39-40½	41-42½	43-44½	45-46½	47-48½
If waist measures	31-32½	33-34½	35-36½	37-38½	39-41	41½-43½
If hips measure	38-39½	40-41½	42-43½	44-45½	46-47½	48-49½

Half Size Patterns Not Necessary

Those of you who have been told that you are a "half size" can take heart that you are no longer locked into such a small selection of patterns. Half size patterns are adjusted for the shorter, fuller busted, shorter waisted woman. However, a quick look at "misses" patterns will show that the location of waistline can be easily adjusted using the foldlines printed on the pattern. On page 77 we have shown you how to adjust the bust dart on a pattern. VOILA! you have a half-size pattern instantly. The only other quickie alteration would be in substracting several inches for the garment's length (check both skirt and sleeves.)

Multi-Sized Patterns Help

The pattern companies are offering fitting help in many forms. There are the multi-sized patterns which allow you to buy a pattern to fit you if you are two sizes different between top and bottom. You simply cut on the appropriate cutting lines for your figure.

Sometimes patterns are sized PETITE, SMALL, MEDIUM, LARGE AND EX-LARGE. Buying these is really tricky, since the pattern design and type of fabric you use will affect the fit. For example, I would always buy a pant pattern in a large, but might buy an unfitted dress or blouse with a loose-fitting sleeve in a medium. I find a lot of inconsistency from pattern to pattern as to what constitutes a SMALL, MEDIUM, AND LARGE. Because of design, I recommend that you flat pattern measure (see page 72) this type of pattern very carefully before cutting to make sure it is large enough.

There are No Absolute Rules

If you decide to ask a salesperson in a fabric store advice regarding your pattern size, please get several opinions. As with the story of the blind man and the elephant, we all see things differently, depending on the point of view. The blind man who had a grasp on the tail thought that the elephant was really skinny! Some people think that clothing should fit loosely, others like a closer fit. You may find that trial and error is the only way to create clothing that is truly comfortable on you.

Make Up a Basic Fit Pattern

Some of us have fit problems that simple alterations won't accommodate. For you, I suggest that you make up a basic fit shell in either muslin or gingham check. All of the pattern companies have patterns with excellent instructions for fitting problem areas. When you make a basic shell, you learn for sure what your best size is in commercial patterns, how your shape varies from the norm.

Once you have learned to fit to your figure, you can easily adapt these adjustments to any other pattern that you choose to make.

The value of using gingham check for your shell can be demonstrated in the drawing below. The check should go around the body parallel to the floor. The vertical checks should be perpendicular to the floor at the center front and center back. Side seams should hang straight down and not swing to the front or back. When the check lines are crooked, or when wrinkles appear these indicate a problem area.

This lady has a sloping shoulder and a high full hip. See what is happening to her checks.

Use Your Fashion Education

It's time to use what you've learned about fashion to select flattering pattern designs that will fit you. Refer to your fashion file for what's "in" and look for similar styles in a pattern book that you could wear and that would duplicate the season's popular looks.

Use what you've learned about line, scale and proportion in the previous chapters. You also shopped ready-to-wear to get a real live view of the newest lines and looks on your body. Keep in mind the items on your "want list" from your closet closeup "toss" session.

Begin by looking in the much-improved "larger figure" pattern book tab. I do feel that we are at a turning point in pattern development, where we will see progress made in the availability of a broader selection of patterns specifically tailored to meet the needs of the larger-figured woman. We should continue to make our desires known to our local merchants, so that our ideas can be communicated to the pattern companies. Or for that matter, write to the company directly, explaining your views about what you feel is missing in pattern catalogs. I really believe that we can create change with comments from the "hinterlands".

Try Specialty Patterns

Besides the major pattern companies, there are several offering special designs. I have found that these patterns offer excellent styles for the larger figure, in that many garments are designed to fit both men and women, so they are amply cut. You can select shirt, coat, drawstring pants and dress patterns.

You might check and see if patterns of this type are available in your area. On the opposite page I am wearing my BIG BLUE BOXCAR COAT (so named by my teenage daughter, who said that is what I looked like wearing it!). It is a padded Japanese fisherman's jacket (Folkwear Patterns) made from Indonesian blue batik, trimmed in navy velvet and lined with bright red chintz. This is definitely an ITEM!

My BIG BLUE BOXCAR COAT uses an ethnic pattern derived from the Japanese fisherman's jacket.

CHAPTER NINE
Make the Pattern Fit You

Okay, we've done our shopping and we've bought the right size pattern. We know which outfit we want to make. We've selected the fabric and notions. But we're a little "iffy" on how to proceed, especially if the pattern that we've chosen is a size 16 to fit our shoulder area and we wear a size 20 on the bottom. RELAX! Soon you'll be using THELEN'S LAW OF CUT AND SEW. But first things first.

I developed THELEN'S LAW many years after I learned how to sew in college home economics classes. In fact, after learning how to sew "right", I gave it up because I found the rules and procedures too tedious.

Let's face it, when you are raising two small children, managing a house, working as a free-lance writer and trying to please a husband, concerns about bound buttonholes and debates over pressing techniques are pale in comparison to everyday life!

But as the years passed and my shape expanded, I returned to my sewing machine with new enthusiasm. This time I was a graduate of the School of Desperation. I was grateful that my sewing skills (though rusty) were functional, because I wanted to make garments that satisfied my desire to dress fashionably in clothing that fit my frame. It worked! I was an overnight success and I am now my own designer/manufacturer of couture clothing!

The Key: Improvise

The key word is IMPROVISE. I would hope by now that I have instilled enough confidence in you that plunging ahead is what you want to do, because rules are only for those who don't have the courage to break them. Palmer and Pletsch always say, "If it works for you, then it must be RIGHT!".

Don't misunderstand: I always buy and fully utilize a pattern. In fact, patterns give me the courage and inspiration to sew. I don't find it incongruous that I rarely follow the directions step-by-step. I don't fault the pattern. My personal style and body shape are the culprits. I just don't seem to conform to the established norm and maybe you don't either. So often in my clothing construction process, I strike a compromise between the pattern ideal and what's workable for me. And that's how THELEN'S LAW was born.

Test a Simple Pattern, Inexpensive Fabric

I suggest that you first try my methods, using a simple pattern and inexpensive material, so that you can experiment with fitting without fear! My techniques might confront those of you who are precise by nature. I am sharing them only in the context that they work for me. You may discover a better technique to accomplish the same thing, once you start playing around with all the possibilities that patterns and fabric present. If you do, please write and share them with me.

We need to take care of several other bits of important business before we begin to sew. First, if there is the slightest possibility that the fabric that you have selected might shrink, please wash it or steam press prior to cutting. Let's face it: Few of us have the knack of shrinking our bodies, so we should stick with clothing that doesn't shrink to fit!

If you used our rules on buying the right size pattern (see page 64) you may find your pattern is smaller than your body measurements below your bustline. Thelen's Law will compensate for the lack of fabric in those areas.

Ease = Wiggle Room

In checking a pattern for fit, we need to remember that ease is needed for the bust, waist, hip and back waist length (see measurement chart page 61 for minimum ease suggestions). Include ease in your measurements in making calculations regarding how much additional fabric you might need to add. Also, ease varies according to the type of pattern and garment that you are making. Obviously, a coat that will be worn over several other layers will need to include extra ease. Pattern companies take this into consideration and automatically add more ease to garments that are worn over other things.

Ease is something that each of us should feel comfortable in adjusting for our own individual figure requirements. We know when a garment feels "good." In *Mother Pletsch's Painless Sewing*, Pati Palmer and Susan Pletsch describe ease as falling into three categories:

COMFORT EASE: The amount agreed on by pattern companies that is comfortable to most individuals.

DESIGN EASE: Ease that is incorporated in a design to give a certain fashion look.

NO EASE: For use when fabrics have built-in ease, such as stretch knits.

I'd like to add a new category of ease:

THELEN EASE: A category especially created for the fuller figure. We can check Thelen Ease in a garment by stretching our arms overhead (does any skin show?), sliding across a car seat (did you rip out the seat of your pants?) and taking off a jacket (was it hard to remove your arms from the sleeves?).

We need close-to-the-body fit just like any other figure shape. But there is no need to live with fit that binds or chafes. Fit your garments for comfortable ease and the inch amounts will no doubt vary for each person. The standards pattern companies set are not absolutes. Feel free to change the ease amounts suggested in the measurement chart!

Two Easy Fitting Techniques

There are two easy steps to fitting insurance before you cut — flat pattern measure and trying on the tissue pattern (a compromise for we who dislike making up muslin fitting shells). Remember to have enough ease or "wiggle room".

Flat Pattern Measure

Flat pattern measuring is an easy way to compare our body size to the pattern size. To do this, lay out the pattern pieces that you will be using. Measure the pattern in the same places that you measured your body, including the minimum ease amounts listed on page 61. This is called "flat pattern measuring". You'll never cut a garment too small if you make this a practice. It's especially important to check the common trouble areas I have starred.

HOW TO FLAT PATTERN MEASURE:

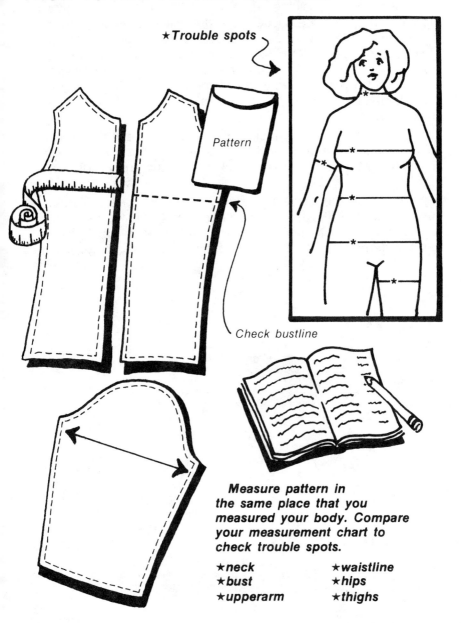

★Trouble spots

Pattern

Check bustline

Measure pattern in the same place that you measured your body. Compare your measurement chart to check trouble spots.

★neck	★waistline
★bust	★hips
★upperarm	★thighs

Try On The Tissue Pattern

Another method to check pattern fit is to pin the tissue together at the shoulders, and sides. If the pattern has a yoke, pin those pieces together too. Leave the side seams open below the bustline. Pin the sleeve seam too, and attach it to the body with one pin at the top.

Clip into the neckline seam so it will curve to your body. Now carefully slip the tissue on and pin it to the center front and center back of your slip or bra, and go to your full length mirror. Could you pin the side seam from bust to hem? (lucky you — that's one place I always need to add!) If not, mark with your marking pen just how much you need to add when you cut. Remember, "ease" too. Mark any other areas that may need extra fabric.

If the pattern has a jacket, it is helpful to pin the jacket together and try it on over the dress (shirt, blouse, pants). By trying the jacket on, you can quickly see if the proportions are right for your shape.

Trying on the tissue can give you a real sense of what a pattern will look like as a finished garment. For me it marks the moment of inspiration or depression! At this point, I rush to cut out the garment, or I fold up the pattern and junk the project!

Now, it's time to BEGIN.

Thelen's Law of Cut and Sew to Fit

All through SEW BIG, I have referred to Thelen's Law as being a cure-all for fitting patterns and sewing garments that can be adjusted to each person's individual requirements.

This concept is not new, nor did I invent it! But I have set it down here for you to use for your convenience. Following these simple steps, you can't go wrong.

Thelen's Law - Step I

Cut it BIG. From the results of trying on the tissue/flat pattern measuring, no doubt you have discovered that you need to add additional inches to have enough fabric to work with in the torso area. The following diagrams show how to do this technique. I always add an extra 2" to the length of the garment too, in case I want to raise the waistline. Also I'm tall and sometimes I need the extra length.

Adding Width

TORSO — Add to side seams, tapering to armhole on front and back.

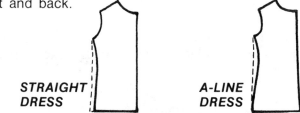

STRAIGHT DRESS *A-LINE DRESS*

TORSO, CHEST AND UPPER ARM — If you are full in all of these areas, use this simple solution: Add same amount to sleeve and bodice front and back. Taper in 6-8" down unless full in arms and waist, then taper further down.

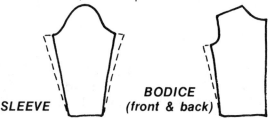

SLEEVE *BODICE (front & back)*

WAIST — Add to side seams, taper to hip.

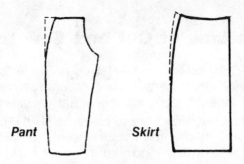

Pant   **Skirt**

Thelen's Law Step II: Pin the seams wrong sides together and try garment on. Now, re-pin to fit if necessary. You must try it on right sides out as your left and right sides may be shaped differently.

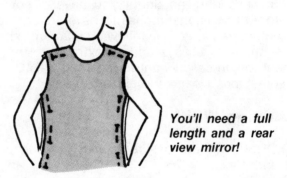

You'll need a full length and a rear view mirror!

Thelen's Law Step III: Take off and mark position of pins so you can un-pin, place seams right sides together, and know where to sew.

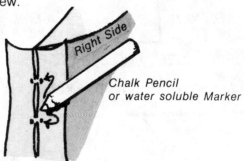

Right Side

Chalk Pencil or water soluble Marker

Thelen's Law Step IV: Now Sew To Fit Your Shape VOILA! A perfect fit that feels good on because you pinned it to fit comfortably to your shape and size.

Here are some simple alterations, if you need to:

Adjust for a Full Bust Line

Patterns are designed for an average B bra cup size. A C cup should have no problem, but a D cup may have to add extra room. A gaping front armhole means you should enlarge bustline.

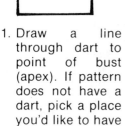
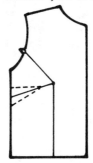
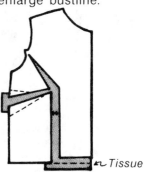

Tissue

1. Draw a line through dart to point of bust (apex). If pattern does not have a dart, pick a place you'd like to have one.

2. Draw a line from waist to apex parallel to grain and then to armhole notch.

3. Cut along lines to but not through armhole. At arrow spread a minimum of ½" for C cup, ¾" for D cup, 1¼" for DD cup.

4. You may need to raise or lower the dart until it points toward your bust point (apex). Add a vertical fitting dart if you want a more fitted look. Old dart is now deeper or you have created a new dart where you slashed and spread your pattern.

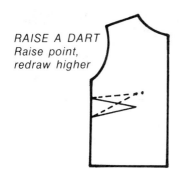

RAISE A DART
_Raise point,
redraw higher_

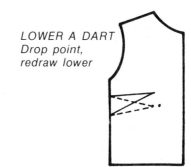

LOWER A DART
_Drop point,
redraw lower_

NOTE: Three added bonuses: your armhole will no longer gap; you will have more width across the bust; you will have more length going over your larger bust and your garment will no longer hike up at bottom in the front.

Add Width for More Comfortable Sleeves

FITTED SLEEVE

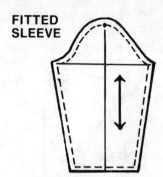 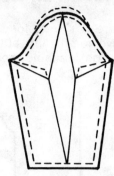

Draw a line down center of sleeve parallel to grain and across from underarm to underarm seam.

Cut on these lines and spread desired amount. If more than 1", redraw original cap.

RAGLAN SLEEVE

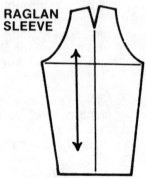 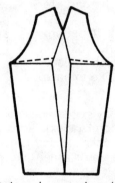

Draw a line down center of sleeve below dart parallel to grain and from underarm to underarm seam.

Cut and spread as in fitted sleeve.

KIMONO SLEEVE

 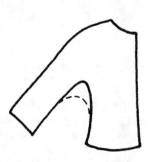

Add to the top . . .

or . . .   cut a deeper armhole.

For Better Shoulder Fit

Since there are three popular sleeve styles that are most comfortable and flattering for larger figures, I want to show how to alter patterns for all three.

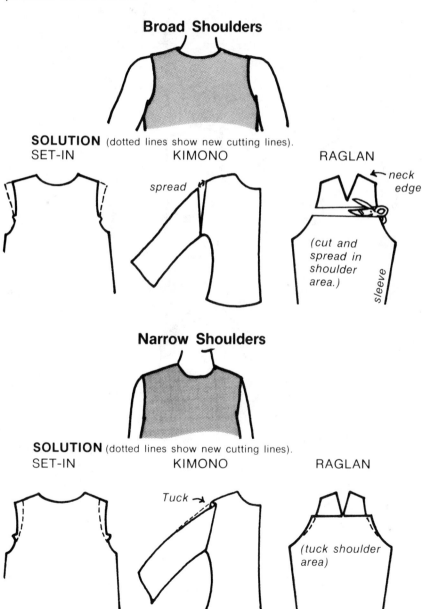

Broad Shoulders

SOLUTION (dotted lines show new cutting lines).

SET-IN KIMONO RAGLAN

spread

← *neck edge*

(cut and spread in shoulder area.)

sleeve

Narrow Shoulders

SOLUTION (dotted lines show new cutting lines).

SET-IN KIMONO RAGLAN

Tuck →

(tuck shoulder area)

Square Shoulders

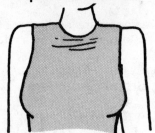

SOLUTIONS (dotted lines show new cutting lines).

SET-IN   KIMONO   RAGLAN
                          (cut off sleeve, move up)

 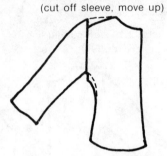 

(make dart shorter and narrower)

Sloping Shoulders

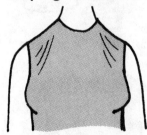

SOLUTIONS (dotted lines show new cutting lines).

SET-IN   KIMONO   RAGLAN
                          (cut off sleeve, move down)

(make dart longer and deeper)

Make a Shoulder Shaper

Often a simple shoulder pad will solve a sloping shoulder problem, squaring the shoulder and creating a more flattering illusion of a smaller torso. The following is a quick, simple method to make a shoulder pad. Make it as thick as you need.

Supplies:

¼ yard fusible knit interfacing (such as Easy-Knit)
¼ yard polyester fleece (Pellon Fleece or Thermolam)

1. Cut a triangle of polyester fleece

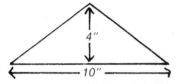

2. If you want additional padding, cut extra layers ½" shorter than the first.

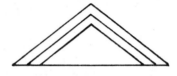

Tip to base (4") is your shoulder width. Change if yours is different.

3. Cut a rectangle of fusible knit and place polyester fleece layers on fusible side of fusible knit.

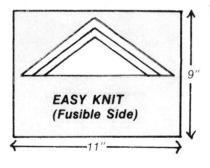

EASY KNIT
(Fusible Side)

4. Fold and fuse edges together using steam iron.

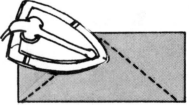

5. Trim away excess fusible knit ¼" from fleece.

6. Tack in place inside garment, the edge of pad should extend ⅜" into sleeve, past sleeve stitching line.

Pant Insurance — Waist, Crotch, Thigh

Often larger figures need more width, crotch depth, and crotch length between the legs (eliminates smiles in the crotch). Add to side seam at hip and waist of pattern whatever amount you determined was needed by flat pattern measuring. For a longer crotch, add an extra 1-2" to the top of the pant and for full thighs add an extra 2-3" to the inseam tapering in just below the knee or above knees if you have slim knees. Mark the original seams, waist, and inseams with chalk or water soluble marking pen as your starting point when pinning or basting a pant together.

pant "insurance"

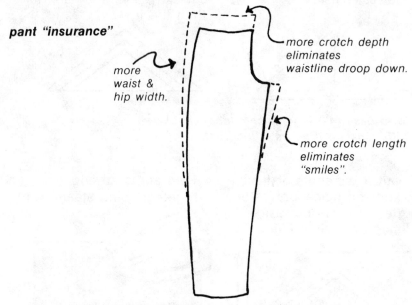

more waist & hip width.

more crotch depth eliminates waistline droop down.

more crotch length eliminates "smiles".

You might think that your garment looks strange with this extra material included, but when you fit it to your body, the garment will take its proper shape . . . YOURS! The trick of applying THELEN'S LAW is that all of the extra fabric can be removed if it isn't needed. By adding the extra fabric in the beginning, we are protecting ourselves from the possibility of not having enough fabric to cover our middle territory where these smaller-size patterns don't allow adequate fabric. THE EXTRA INCHES ARE INSURANCE, and they could turn out to be the best investment you ever made!

CHAPTER TEN

Cut, Sew and Individualize

Have the Right Tools

I believe in having the right tools to do the job. I relied on the Palmer/Pletsch *Painless Sewing* book to lay out my sewing area, after experiencing years of disorganization. My mugrack display of sewing tools right above my machine saves me a lot of wear and tear, but I admit that I don't use a paper bag to catch my scraps, since I sew with such wild abandon!

I have invested in an excellent iron (Sunbeam Shot-of-Steam®) and am presently considering shifting over from the ironing board to a tabletop pressing board. But I feel like I've made a lot of progress already, since, for years, I'd been walking to another room to press, never thinking to shift my ironing board to my sewing area. (Really dumb!)

Be Professional

Because you'll never know when you need to sew, an in-house supply of notions really makes sense. When I want to make something up and wear it out the door a couple of hours later, there's no time to rush out and buy findings.

Besides, I feel that it's part of the home sewer's role to run a professional shop. Our finished garment reflects the effort that we've put into making it. Having all the right tools and notions contribute to a fine finish.

It's my practice to have everything that I need to start sewing on hand, and that means spending money on trim, thread, interfacings, etc., in advance. You might wonder how I know what I would need, or how I could match the thread; but here is a basic stash that we can accumulate and draw upon fairly successfully. I keep the following on hand.

1. Variety of threads in color, weight, type
2. Three sizes of scissors: cutting, trimming, embroidery
3. Basic seam finishes: hem tape, lace edging, bias tape
4. Trims: laces, crocheted edges, rickrack, braids
5. Buttons: special ones in brass, horn, neutrals that work on any fabric or color, such as pearl
6. Interfacings

RECOMMENDED INTERFACINGS

	FUSIBLE	NON-FUSIBLE
LIGHT	Easy-Knit® Sheer-weight Pellon®	Armo-Press Soft® Sheer-weight Pellon®
MEDIUM	Easy-Shaper® Sof-Shape®	Veri-form Durable Press®
HEAVY ENOUGH!	Pelaire® Armo-Weft®	Acro® or P-1® Hair Canvas®

Ask an Expert

I think of my fabric salesperson as the "expert" on what's new. On her suggestion, I try out new notions. That's how I discovered the marking pen with water-soluble ink. It changed my life! This pen is perfect for pattern alteration. With it, you can easily mark directly on the fabric, while wearing the garment or with it off the body. I draw all over my garments when I am using THELEN'S LAW OF CUT AND SEW. Then I simply dissolve the evidence with a dab of water. It sure beats chalk or tailor tacks.

Every time I go in the fabric store, I find something new. I recently invested in a point turner and a bodkin. Not new, but new to me. Next trip, I'm going to purchase a product called Fray Check®, an anti-raveler that you can add to seam edges to cut down on sewing time.

There's also a new product called "Seams Great®". It's precut strips of nylon tricot that can be used for binding the seams of unlined garments. It gives you a fine finishing effect with the plus of controlling raveling.

It's "in fashion" to have the latest notions. You can't successfully play the game without the tools and the knowledge of how to use them. Spending money on patterns, fabric, and notions is a big responsibility, especially in these times when values are fluctuating. It's our obligation to spend wisely and to stretch our dollars as far as we can. However, when we decide to dress "fashionably", we know that it will require some purchases each season to win the fashion game.

Cutting Out

I use a sharp, lightweight pair of shears that I keep hidden from my family, who would like to use them for cutting everything from cardboard to leather. And I use a heavy cardboard cutting board that I lay out on our carpeted living room floor. I work on the floor, rather than on a tabletop, since I like to stretch all the fabric that I have out at once to experiment with different fabric layouts. On the table, everything tends to fall off the edge.

There are several tools that I use to make cutting easier. I've started using longer, glass-headed pins that I keep in a large pin cushion. I just graduated from using regular pins that I stored in a box and spilled regularly . . . grrrr.

Don't Cut Too Many Things At Once!

A word of caution: I've found that if I've cut too many patterns out at once, several never get finished. Right now I have at least five cut-out garments languishing away in a box, and I fear that both fashion and my figure have by-passed them. So the rule of thumb is to cut out only what you want to wear . . . preferably the next day.

Now we have a cut-out, altered pattern, and it's time to sit down and sew. I believe in beginning with CONVICTION. My firm resolve stems from all the time that I've spent studying colors, clothes and trends. I KNOW what I like. And in the case of the garment that I'm making, I LOVE the design. I LOVE the fabric. And I know that this particular garment is going to look GREAT on me. Strangely, I find that the patterns that are still in pieces in the closet somehow failed in one of these areas.

Marking

I prefer to pin fabric to pattern, rather than using pattern weights, since I like to transfer markings as I sew, rather than at the time of cutting. I know that there is the suggestion that it is easier to "sew in the flow," when everything is pre-marked but, frankly, I need to work with each piece as I'm ready to use it. (Using Thelen's Law, a lot of pattern marking is a waste of time, since the location of darts, gathers, pockets, etc., may be changed or eliminated altogether from the finished product.)

Getting Motivated to Sew

Some people tell me that they consciously spend time visualizing their projected wardrobe. Try spending 20 minutes on the couch, picturing how great you will look in the garment you are about to make . . . where will you wear it? How good will it feel on your body? How will you accessorize it? How will it coordinate within your wardrobe? Give this exercise a try on days when you can't seem to get up the steam you need to start sewing.

Before beginning to sew, I set up my ironing board and prepare my steam iron for action. I put up the pattern directions on the wall in front of me and assemble needed notions and tools. Taking a deep breath, I sit down at the machine.

Sewing is Improvising

After I sew the fronts and backs together, I try the garment on and proceed to the full-length mirror, taking pins and trusty water-soluble marking pen in hand. IT'S THE MOMENT OF TRUTH. This is when I will determine which of the pattern details will survive.

You may find that a pattern you selected was not as flattering to you as you expected. I also double-check fit. Is everything comfortable? Improvising is a way to salvage anything you sew if you just remember the options you have and are a little daring.

At this point, I can see how the fabric drapes or hold its shape. I check the darts, pleats, gathers, tucks, zippers and buttonholes. ARE THEY NEEDED? WHAT DO THEY ADD BESIDES A LOT OF EXTRA WORK?

Where to Improvise

The following are improvising examples:

Skirt — take out any fullness . . . add slit?

Or you might try changing the width of a skirt or pant legs. Sometimes I can see that several soft pleats would look better than the bunchy gathers that the pattern calls for across shoulders or stomach. The type of fabric being used definitely affects the way a design should be adapted. Obviously, soft jersey drapes better than heavier velour, and you can use more fabric on the body. What the heavier silhouette doesn't want is BULK. If the fabric/pattern gives a bulky look, I simply whack it out. I certainly don't need to pad my paunch!

Pockets — do I want them? Right location? Size?

Neckline — do I like it? Take off the collar? Does it fit?

Tucks/darts — do I need any? Or remove any?

Sleeves — what length do I like? Too full?

Shoulder line — if it droops or pulls adjust the seams.

Armhole — I double check the fit. Is everything comfortable?

If I find that the armhole is small, I might lower it ¼"-½". This won't affect the sleeve as there is usually enough ease in the cap to protect you. If not, lower the underarm after the sleeve is set in.

IMPROVISING — I used a maternity pattern for this tunic, which can be worn as a jumper or layered over pants.

Sleeve-cap — This adjustment is a matter of personal taste. It doesn't affect fit at all. I think that fullness across the top of the sleeve cap (shoulder), as in the case of "puffed sleeves," isn't flattering to larger figure shapes unless the fabric is very soft or you are very young.

If you bought a garment like this or found a pattern you loved in every way except that it had puffy sleeves, you can remove the fullness as you sew.

In both cases, I take the sleeve as it's originally shaped and pin it into the armhole, starting at the bottom seam juncture. As I work toward the top (shoulder line), from back and front, I move the sleeve fabric up over the armhole seam until I can pin the sleeve into the armhole without gathering. When I have finished, I may have removed as much as 2 inches of excess fabric. I trim the sleeve cap, leaving a ⅝" seam and stitch into the armhole.

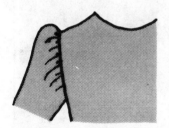  

PROBLEM:
Puffy sleeve cap.

SOLUTION:
Remove
excess fabric.

RESULT:
Smooth
shoulder.

An optional method to flatten or control the puffiness is to press the upper two-thirds of the sleeve seam toward the bodice and topstitch.

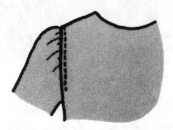

Length — There are a few guidelines to keep in mind when changing length. Longer pants add length to your silhouette. Straight skirts can be worn shorter than long soft skirts, but my recommendation is NO KNEES. Shorter people have to be careful of skirts that are too long and appear overwhelming. Remember the most important question is "how does it look on *you*?"

Waistlines — raise/lower/eliminate?
My figure is sort of rectangular. I really don't have a waistline, so I prefer not to accentuate that fact. If I am making a dress to be worn without a jacket, I adjust the pattern so that the waistline falls just below the bustline, perhaps with a tie in the back for fit. This line gives me a close fit in the upper portion of my body and allows the fabric to softly fall over the lower two-thirds of my figure. If I'm making a style with a jacket, I can wear a belted garment underneath as only a small section down the front will show. Another line that I like for dresses is the blouson style — fabric bloused over a narrow belt.

To establish the illusion of a fitted waistline look over my thicker middle, I often belt and add a jacket worn open in the front. Straight on, I have the tailored look of separates. And from the side and in back my jacket covers the fuller portion of my silhouette. If *you* have a waistline that you feel is worthy of show, then by all means choose styles that fit in that area.

With the unfitted dress, my feeling is that "no waistline" dresses should be well-fitted through the shoulders and bustline, and then flaring to the hem for a sweep to the skirt that is feminine and flattering.

Warning: Drastic Changes Might Occur!

Sometimes, at the very last, if the design porportions look wrong, I make drastic changes. It's amazing how taking out some fullness in a skirt will alter the balance of the sleeve in relationship to the bodice of a garment. So when you change one part of a garment, recheck your total look. Usually, when you slim down a skirt, everything has to slim down a bit.

I once made an evening outfit where top and bottom were elasticized at the waist to give a blouson effect. In theory it worked, but in reality the outfit got drafty whenever I raised my arms. I took out the elastic and sewed the pieces together. I wear it sashed at the new waistline, blousing the top and I love it.

And be aware of how your garment fits when you move. Can you sit comfortably. Move your arms? Is the length right when you are sitting down? When I add a slit, does it gap in all the wrong places?

Keep The Seam Ripper In Hand — It's Worth It

I feel that I've had to toss the rule book out because my body doesn't conform to any of the rules. When I sit down to restitch my garment, I may repeat the process two or three times. Each time after I stitch, I return to the mirror and, with trusty pencil and pins, I try the garment on again. Often I know the look that I want, but I'm not sure how to get the effect, so I nip in a little here and there. So much of the garment's fit depends on the fabric you make it from. I can make the same pattern in several fabrics and end up with entirely different garments.

Easy Ways to Rip:

METHOD 1. Cut stitches with seam ripper every inch on one side of seam. Pull thread on other side. Brush off or pull out small clipped threads.

METHOD 2. Pull seam apart then CAREFULLY cut stitches. Don't force it. When the seam ripper gets hung up, pull seam apart again. It's safer with ball side of seam ripper down. Do not use this method on fine silks or knits.

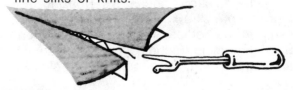

Finishing Touches

How much time and effort a person spends on finishing a garment is a personal thing. Some people pride themselves on their buttonholes, hems and seam finishes. I'm a trim and accessories woman myself, preferring to concentrate on the dramatic effect that the outside of the garment makes, rather than to know that the construction is a work of art. You might feel just the opposite, though.

To Thine Own Self Be True

Finishing a garment is how we put our personal stamp on it. It's what makes your garment original, instead of a good "imitation." If you get any inspiration at all from this book, I hope it helps to motivate you beyond trying to duplicate a pattern EXACTLY.

To copy fashion looks today, I feel creative sewing is the answer . . . Thelen's Law gives you the right to control how the pattern, fabric and design fit your figure. The same goes for RTW. Don't consider a garment "sacred" in its original form. Often, it doesn't take much to upgrade an outfit's fashion rating. Are you satisfied with the quality of the buttons? Often I upgrade. On my natural raw silk blazer, I added grey pearl buttons, removing the cream plastic ones. Consider closing a handsewn jacket with a piece of jewelry or adding self-fabric ties in place of buttons.

Each person can easily discover what sewing skills and methods work for them by simply starting to sew. If you are not satisfied with your results, get more help, but never consider your efforts failures simply because your garment didn't meet your expectations. To create fashionable, flattering clothing, you will have to experiment. By the sheer nature of becoming more creative, you can expect a few disasters along the way.

CHAPTER ELEVEN
Coping with Changing Size

*It must have been
something I ate!*

I consider the ability to alter garments as important as a person's ability to sew. Why? Because a larger person's weight often fluctuates, and it may be necessary for us to alter a garment from season to season to achieve proper fit.

Another reason for understanding alteration is that sometimes I find a ready-to-wear garment that fits some parts of me, but not all, yet is exactly what I want to add to my wardrobe. It is practical to alter the too-small garment if it's inexpensively priced or is such a perfect addition to be worth the time.

Gussets — The Great Expanders!

The gusset is the most useful alteration that I know about for larger figures. A gusset is a piece of fabric that is inserted into the underarm seams where bodice and set-in sleeve meet. It adds ease to the upper arm, armhole and bustline areas. If you have very full arms, even large size ready-to-wear is often too tight in the sleeve.

I can point to many treasured garments in my closet that would have long ago been tossed had it not been for the GUSSET. It can be used in a ready-made or hand-sewn garment that has become too tight or it can be added while sewing. For example, if I have already cut out a pattern that has set-in sleeves and I find it uncomfortable after the first fitting, I can add a gusset for a softer, fuller line. I've even used a gusset in a pant crotch for the treatment of "thighus gigantus." If you begin to see smiles in the crotch of your pants, it may be the only answer. Wear a long top if the gusset shows.

Material for making the gusset (which will show) must be "borrowed" from the garment if it is ready-made. If the garment is handsewn, hopefully you have kept a scrap of the fabric. When I have to "borrow", I use the self-fabric tie belt or an inside pocket to make the gusset. I might also be able to match the garment to a purchased piece of fabric. Add a gusset following these easy steps:

1. Open the underarm seam of the too-small garment and try it on. Measure or "guestimate" the size of the opening. Add 1" to the length and 1" to the width of the opening. Cut a diamond shaped gusset to fit the opening.

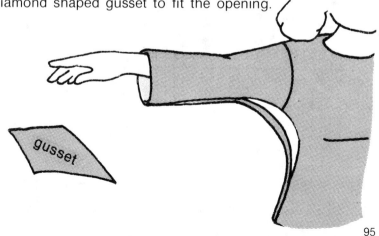

2. Working from the inside of the garment, pin or baste the gusset in place to the four seam junctures and then to the seam allowances on all four sides of the gusset. Note that the gusset extends ½″ beyond the opening at the junctures since you cut it 1″ longer and wider than necessary.

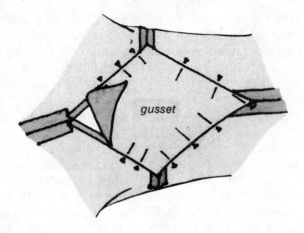

gusset

3. Now try on the garment to see if the gusset is too bunchy or too large. You might need to re-shape it by taking in the seams. Sometimes I take in one end more than the other or shorten the gusset at both ends.

I play with it until the gusset is basically invisible, in that it is merely filling in the gap where I needed ease but isn't "bunchy". This isn't a very scientific method because each garment demands its own solution.

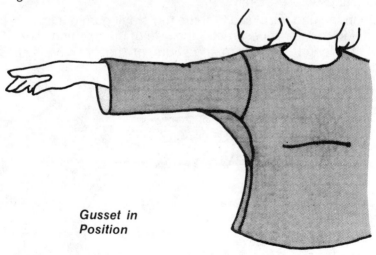

Gusset in Position

4. From the inside, stitch gusset to seam allowances. In addition, you may want to topstitch around edges for extra strength.

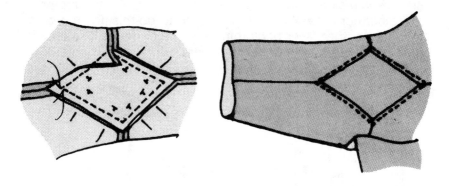

Short Sleeves that are Too Tight

Short sleeves that are too tight in the upper arm can be slit open either in the underarm seam where it won't show or on the top where the slit would have to be faced. If the short sleeve is gathered into a band that is too tight, remove the band. You may then add a nice touch by slitting the sleeve open and tying the sleeve ends together.

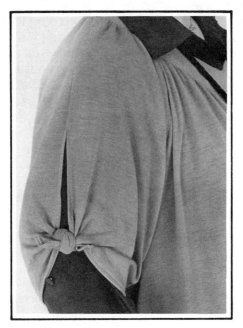

Making the Armhole Larger

Enlarging the armhole on a garment with or without sleeves is a simple trick that we can use to make the armhole more comfortable. You may also need to do this if you decide to wear another layer of clothing under a garment. The procedure is simple. Stitch underarm seam ¼" lower at a time, trim seam to ¼", and try on. Stitch another ¼" lower and trim if it is still too tight.

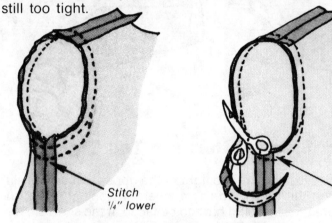

Stitch
¼" lower

Trim seam
to ¼"

Lengthening the Crotch of Pants

Have you ever gained weight and noticed your pants became tighter in the crotch? For more room lower the crotch seam in the same way as the underarm seam above. Turn one leg inside out and put the other leg inside it. Sew minimum adjustments of ¼" at a time, trim to ¼", and try on the pants until you are satisfied. CAUTION! You may have to buy flatter shoes as you are making the legs shorter as well!

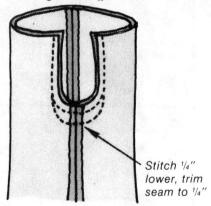

Stitch ¼"
lower, trim
seam to ¼"

Let Out the Side Seams

This is often easier said than done as you may not have enough seam allowance to be of any help. In that case, you can split open the seam, overlay a band of trim, and edgestitch the trim in place. There is, however, a fine line between tacky and tasteful in doing this. Choose a trim that blends in both color and style with the fabric.

To a lovely satin evening outfit that I wanted to save, I opened up the side seams of the top including the underarm seam of the sleeve and added a band of heavy cotton lace. I also opened up the outside seams of the pants and ran the same lace down the sides. It added both evening glamour plus inches!

Shirt and pants show side seam overlays that are both decorative and serve the purpose of enlarging the clothes.

Add Width by Conversion

The absolutely all-time easiest alteration is to convert a garment from double breasted to single breasted, which means taking off all of the buttons and throwing half of them away. Try on the garment and position the buttons in a single row according to how it fits you best.

This works especially well for coats or raincoats with raglan sleeves. I searched long and hard for an off-white trenchcoat because I felt I didn't have the sewing skills to make one. I finally found one — SIZE 16 — double breasted. Now it is a size 20, single breasted! Just remember double breasted and wraps have potential expansion room.

Even simpler is the don't-button-it-at-all alteration. From season to season, you may find that what buttoned last year won't this year. If you've gained weight, go through your closet and see if you can salvage anything by wearing it without buttons over another garment. For example, wear a coatdress as a topper over another dress in layered fashion. Convert garments into ITEMS to wear over sundresses.

Slits Create Room

Slits are a girl's best friend if she's large. I slit the side seams on almost everything that I buy, because very few garments give me enough tummy room when they fit in the shoulders. I also slit clothes I want to wear when I fluctuate in weight.

A straighter garment with a slit for room to move is often more flattering than one that is very full. For example, a shirt that is slit on the sides gives a straighter line than one that is full, billowing out from a yoke. Straight skirts are often more slenderizing to the eye than lots of fabric gathered into a dirndle. But how to walk — how to sit? SLITS are the answer, but I suggest that you add your slits on the side or in the rear of your garment. None of us has legs that are so good looking that we want to put a full-page ad out front!

I converted my double-breasted trenchcoat into a single-breasted style by removing a row of buttons and I gained 4 inches of ease.

Slits are also a key in layering as they create a vertical line. Note the slit in the jumper on page 25.

And regarding slits and slips! I put my skirts with slits on and put on a regular slip underneath. Then, snip the slip so it has a slit in the same place. I finish the edges in foldover lace. So far, all my slits have worked with the same slip. P.S. If you have too-short slips (and I think most large women do, since our bodies take up more garment width than length), it's simple to lengthen them with strips of lace. Add as many rows as you need. I purposely have one slip that is too long that I wear FOR SHOW!

Eliminate A Waistband For Comfort

Are you no-waisted? Most fuller figures are, but what to do about it. One trick is to remove uncomfortable, stiff waistbands from skirts and pants. In their place I stitch in a band of men's waistbanding (available in notions departments) releasing any darts or gathers needed for additional ease. This is the procedure:

1. Remove existing waistband.
2. On right side of garment, pin strip of waistbanding in place, right sides together. Stitch ¼ inch from fabric edge all around waistline. Clip and turn band to inside of garment. Press and flatten edge with wooden pressing block.
3. Topstitch ¼ inch from edge around waistline. Press again.

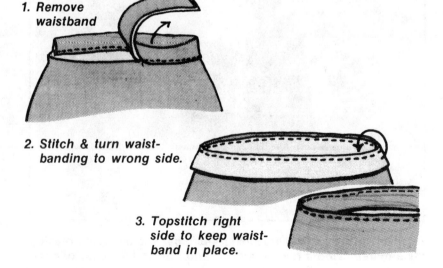

1. Remove waistband

2. Stitch & turn waistbanding to wrong side.

3. Topstitch right side to keep waistband in place.

I call this a "natural" waistband treatment. You'll notice that this "natural" waistline rides about 2" lower on your torso. Actually, our additional poundage often makes us officially "short-waisted". For this reason, remember to use narrower elastic (½-¾") in pull-on pants and skirt waistband, also.

When It's Too Big . . .

I haven't mentioned alterations for garments that are too large. I feel strongly that large figures shouldn't masquerade as moving tents; so I always remove as much excess fabric as I can from garments that are too large, unless the fabric is very soft.

There are no special techniques involved. For fitting boxy blazers, I rely on long darts on either side of the center back seam. Sometimes I take in the side back seams or side seams a little.

Lately, I have been narrowing my pantlegs in keeping with fashion's direction. Since my legs are full, I'm not going to peg in the bottom too much, but a slight narrowing from the knee on down gives a slimmer look.

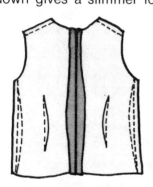 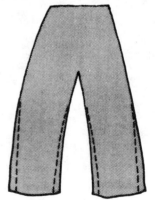

It Takes Moxie!

Alterations are made of the same stuff that straight sewing consists of — a minimum amount of technique and a maximum amount of MOXIE!

Anyone can find clothes to wear, but dressing a larger figure fashionably takes cunning. It gives me a lot of pleasure to buy a size 16 dress to fit my shoulders and know that soon I'll be wearing it on the rest of my body which is a size 20 looking every bit as glamorous as the designer intended — MAYBE EVEN MORE SO!

CHAPTER TWELVE
Great Items!

Simplicity is the key to ITEMS. Let the fabric tell the story as in this paisley chintz jacket.

You probably noticed one of my favorite ITEMS when you purchased your copy of SEW BIG. I am wearing my lavish lace tunic over black evening pyjamas. Together they make an ITEM. ITEMS add sparkle to a tired wardrobe. Without them, the clothes that you wear will lack your personal stamp.

Remember these 4 characteristics of an ITEM:

- They are always unusual and unexpected
- They are made from fantastic fabrics or are uniquely crafted from other materials
- They are timeless treasures, regardless of their monetary value
- They perfectly reflect personal taste

It's a treat for me to show you some of my ITEMS. I'd love it if you would send me photos of some ITEMS that you've collected, either special clothing or accessories. An old-timer in my closet is the golden drapery cord that I purchased in a fabric store (see page 107).

Stay alert. You never know where you'll discover an ITEM. I wear 3 handblown electrical glass insulators on a gold chain. They look like mini clear glass donuts and make great toys for my fingers to play with during the day. My husband found them in a junkshop, and I found them in his tool box!

ITEMS can be handsewn by YOU. The following are some patterns for quickie clothing. What I like about these designs is that they make comfortable, unique and easy to sew clothing.

Genie Jeans

Now YOU may never wear Genie Jeans, but I've found that they are fun and comfortable, especially in warm weather. Wouldn't it be great to surprise your friends by wearing something crazy like this?

I recommend soft, drapable fabrics — challis, gauze, crepe de chine, tissue faille. NOTE: I didn't have satisfactory results when I tried soft light-weight knits. The fabric didn't have enough body to drape without clinging.

To make, purchase the following:

Fabric: 2 yards of 45" fabric.

Optional Lining: 2 yards of 45" lining (use in see-through fabrics).

Notions: 4 yards of ¼" grosgrain ribbon, matching thread.

A hidden plus!!! When you tire of the Genie Jeans — turn your 2 yards of fabric into another garment!

Unlined — Turn ⅜" to wrong side on selvage edges. Edgestitch. Fold 1" to wrong side on each end and turn under ¼" on the raw edge and topstitch. Thread ½" ribbon or cord through casing.

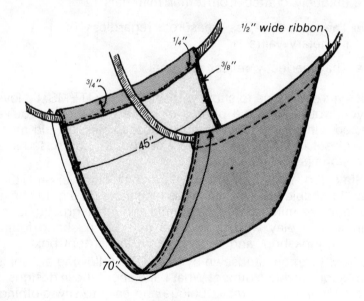

Shown is combination of the GENIE JEANS and the TRICKY TABARD (short version). The jeans are made of rayon challis, while the tabard is velvet. The gold cord purchased in a fabric store is a lengthening casual accessory.

Lined — Place lining and fashion fabric right sides together and stitch ⅜" seam on long selvage edges. Turn and press. Finish as in unlined version.

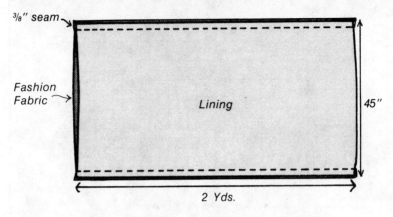

Two yards of fabric makes ankle-length pants on me. (Remember, I'm 5 feet 8 inches). If you need shorter "jeans", adjust the yardage used. Get out some yardage that you have on hand and experiment before you sew.

You can use wider fabric if it is lightweight enough to gather nicely. I wouldn't try getting by with 36-inch widths unless you want a lot of leg to show.

To wear; place fabric on the floor. Step over the middle and pull up the front end. Tie in the back, gathering the width of material to cover the front and sides of thighs. Reach down and bring up back edge, again adjusting gathering to cover sides of legs overlapping the front panel, and tying in the front.

Caftan Coat

This garment looks wonderful in wool to wear as you would a cape, in raw silk, printed crepe de chine for evening, or in a graphic design cotton as a daytime wrap. You will need the following:

Fabric: 2½ yards of 45" fabric
Notions: Matching thread

NOTE: Caftan length can be altered by using wider or narrower widths of fabric. Width of garment will be altered by increasing or decreasing amount of yardage used.

1. Fold length of fabric in half, right sides together. Stitch 18" down from one edge, using ⅝" seam. VARIATION: To bring more fullness to the front of the garment when worn, stitch 9" from edge instead. This gives beachrobes and bathrobes more front over lap.

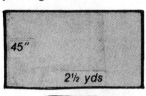

2. Position seam at center.

3. Press center seam open and pin across top as shown, then stitch top edges together, using a ⅝" seam.

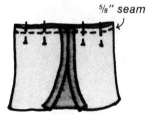

4. From shoulder seam, slit armholes 9" deep. Stitch a hand or machine rolled hem around all raw edges. Head goes here at X.

Unusual fabrics such as this great subtle stripe raw silk make great CAFTAN COATS!

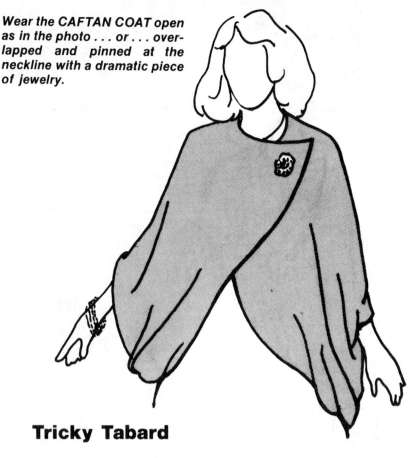

Wear the CAFTAN COAT open as in the photo . . . or . . . overlapped and pinned at the neckline with a dramatic piece of jewelry.

Tricky Tabard

Tabards are great for layering with interesting fabrics and for camouflaging. They are open at the sides, but secured with ties or button tabs. I have made tabards for both dress and sportswear, once using a pink panne velvet and another time a wool tweed, and another in denim. The pattern is a great remnant user-upper as well.

The size of the tabard can be altered to fit the fabric available and also to customize each individual body. I recommend cutting out a paper or Pellon pattern and trying out various sleeve and body lengths. I will give you dimensions for a variety of lengths.

You will need:

Fabric: 1¼, 1½ or 2 yards of 36" or 45" fabric - depending on the length you choose.

Optional lining: the same amount if you choose to line to the edge.

Notions: matching thread.

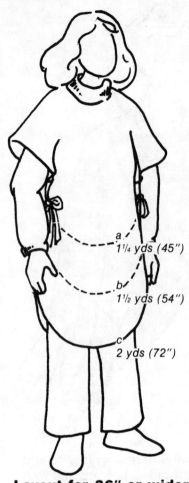

To Sew the Tricky Tabard:

Unlined:
Cut and hand roll hem and neckline! That's all!!

a.
1¼ yds (45")

b.
1½ yds (54")

c.
2 yds (72")

OR
Lined: Sew outside edges together, clip, and press. Finish neck opening by hand rolling a hem through both layers.

Layout for 36" or wider fabric

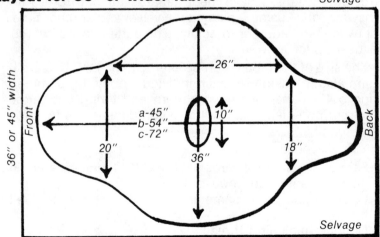

Selvage

Front

Back

36" or 45" width

26"

a-45"
b-54"
c-72"

10"

20"

18"

36"

Selvage

Quickie Pants to Wear with Your "ITEMS"

Here's the pant to wear with a long tabard where only the bottom half of the leg shows. If you have a basic pant pattern, use it for this quick and easy no-side-seam pull-on pant. It takes less than an hour to make.

Lap outside seams of front and back pattern pieces. If your pattern doesn't have a casing, add 3″ to top above waistline.

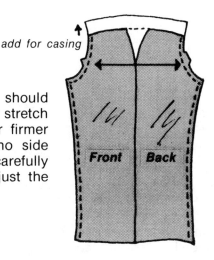

add for casing

Measure hipline. Pattern should be same size as your body for stretch knits and up to 2″ larger for firmer wovens. (Because there is no side seam, you need to measure carefully as you won't be able to adjust the width.)

Sew inseams, right sides together. Press open.

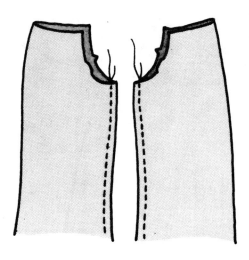

Turn one leg inside out and put the other leg inside. Stitch the crotch seam. Trim lower third to ¼" and stitch again to reinforce.

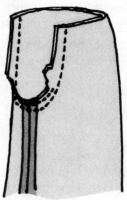

Make elastic casing by turning top edge to the inside 1½" and stitching a 1¼" casing. Wrap 1" elastic around your waist until comfortable. Allow 1" for overlap. Holding onto elastic at one end, insert the other end through casing, pin ends together. Try on pants to test elastic size. Adjust elastic until comfortable, stitch ends together by machine. Hem by machine or by hand.

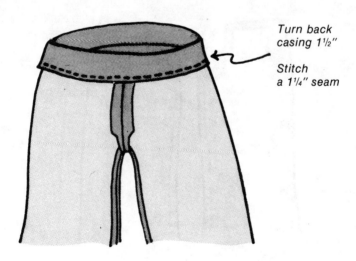

Turn back casing 1½"

Stitch a 1¼" seam

Capes

I feel that large women can wear capes better than small women because they are not overpowered by them. The pattern companies have some great cape patterns such as the one featured below. Capes are also less restrictive than coats.

photo courtesy McCall's Patterns

Sweaters Are ITEMS

Sweaters are super-important. I like them because they layer well, they can be taken off and on during the day, and they are always comfortable. My "ITEMS" include several full-length cardigan sweaters and a hand-knit work-of-art sweater of natural yarns. I also like to wear jersey-like turtlenecks under my shirts during cool weather.

Scarves — Find the Right Size

Scarf size is important to us. The squares that I use average 26 inches, and the rectangles average 70 inches by 12 inches. All the scarves I wear are very soft fabric; silk, silk blends, knits (some with metallic threads). My shawls (54 inches square) are sheer challis of wool or rayon. I have one silk shawl (50 inches square).

I mention specific size because large figures demand accessories that are in scale with silhouette shape, as well as the styling of the clothing being worn. A little bitty scarf (14 inches) tied around my neck makes the rest of me look larger. A too-small shawl that barely drops below my bust draws attention to my shape, instead of complementing my whole costume.

To discover the optimum size you should wear, take a 60" square of fabric. Fold it on the diagonal like you would wear a shawl, and put it around your shoulders. Did you disappear? If so, the square is too large. Cut it down 5 inches and try again, reducing the size in 5-inch increments until you feel comfortable and find the look flattering on you.

Then take a smaller square (30 inches) and tie it around your neck. Does it obscure the front of your outfit — is your face and neck lost? Too large again. Cut it down to your size.

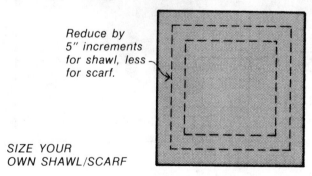

Reduce by 5" increments for shawl, less for scarf.

SIZE YOUR
OWN SHAWL/SCARF

A sheer wool challis shawl beats the winter chill and makes a great "ITEM" with the right trim.

Now try a rectangle. Often I wear a long scarf that hangs down to my knees (for me that's about 80 inches). I make mine about 8" wide. Again, experiment for yourself. The value of wearing a scarf of this type is the longer line that it adds to the silhouette.

Fabric type will determine a lot about the dimensions of a scarf. If you want to make a shawl of a bulky fabric, you would want to use only one thickness, making a triangle instead of a square. You could finish the raw edge with a rolled hem or fringe.

Sometimes it's fun to make reversible scarves, so that you can show two colors or two textures. You might want to reverse the fabric faces for a shiny/dull combination. One of the greatest scarves is one made of a paisley challis. It can be wonderfully tied over a solid color dress. Finish edges of scarves you make by stitching ¼" from the edge and fringing or do a hand or machine rolled hem.

Buy Comfortable Shoes

Fashion often spotlights shoe styles that make heavy demands on the body. Four-inch spike heels don't offer a larger woman the support her body needs to walk comfortably. I compromise by choosing shoe shapes that are popular and maintain a consistent heel height (no more than 2¾"). For day-wear, I choose shoes with good arch support and cushiony sole construction. Although they are harder to put on, I like sandals, but slip-on pumps, which are easy to get into, always look nice. Pass on ankle straps unless you have slim legs.

Jewelry Adds Jazz

Because we wear jewelry mostly to focus attention on our face, we must carefully examine our facial features to establish the type and size of jewelry that will be most flattering.

I have long ad mired Bea Arthur (TV's "Maude") and am tempted to copy her style of dressing right down to her chunky jewelry, but my features are more delicate than hers. My face is overwhelmed when surrounded by large earrings, several strands of big beads and bangle bracelets on both arms. Many large women can go Maude's route, but an alternative is DRA-MATIC JEWELRY — which doesn't always mean large. Important pieces! But don't overdo it. Strive for accents that frame the face. Sometimes monumental drop or large button earrings are in order, but if you feel yourself disappearing behind all the glitter, it's not for you.

I chose a beautiful lapel pin and a stunning silk scarf. For this outfit, adding a necklace and drop earrings would shatter the look of controlled elegance.

CHAPTER THIRTEEN
Fashion is Fun . . .
and It's for Every Body!

FASHION IS FUN, when you wear ITEMS like this Moroccan hooded dress, topped with a heavy cotton cape printed with American Indian designs. These two boldly patterned pieces work together because it's a story in black, white and brown.

Up to this point, we've been talking about getting organized, sewing, altering, pulling a workable wardrobe together. Now it's time we switched to the BIG PICTURE and talked about how fashion affects the way that we feel about ourselves, and how we can upgrade our personal appearance to complement what we have learned about fashionable dressing.

Putting on great-looking outfits won't work miracles, although it's bound to help if, inside and outside, the rest of "us" is in shambles. Up till now, we may not have been aware that our image is a top-to-bottom/inside-outside thing.

Let me make it clear that I'm not advocating any hard-and-fast rules about how a woman can make herself look more attractive, because we can agree that "beauty is in the eye of the beholder." Even the definition of "attractive" is open for debate! I don't think that anyone has to be physically "beautiful" to get a STAR rating. What is important is a person's commitment to good grooming habits and proper wardrobe maintenance.

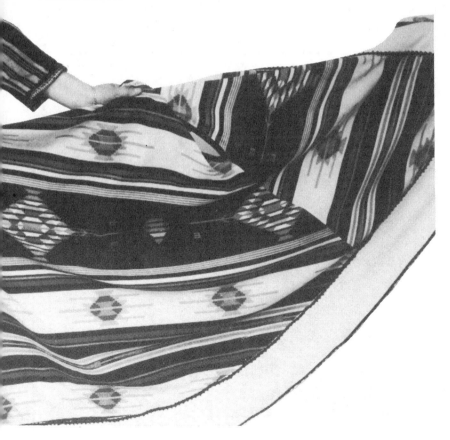

I feel that my overall appearance is enhanced by a flattering hairstyle (and clean hair of course!) Fashion sets up certain guidelines, but always face shape is the key factor in choosing a hairstyle. And pick a cut that you can manage, unless you have unlimited time and money to spend on upkeep. I recently found that I couldn't cope with a blow-dry haircut, even though I had spent a fortune on special brushes, a hand dryer, and a fancy mirror. I am a whiz with a body perm and hot curlers, so now I carefully choose a style that can be maintained in this manner. Still, if fashion cried, BRAIDS, I might add one here or there for effect.

Regarding cosmetics: In the process of producing this book, I became an "instant model." My photographer, Carole Day (herself a professional model) made up my face prior to our photographic sessions, showing me tricks for highlighting my eyes and contouring my face. The "before" and "after" proved to me that a model's pretty face is no more natural than her skinny shape!

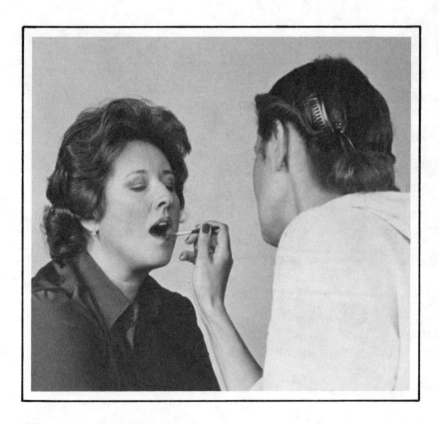

I can't tell you how to apply makeup, since I'm still in the "practice-in-the-bathroom" stage myself, but I do mention a great book on the subject in the Fashion Bibliography. Also, I heartily recommend that you take advantage of the free makeup sessions that department stores feature to sell cosmetics, or if you are shy about being a public model, make an appointment for a facial and makeup session with a specialist in your area. (Check the phone book Yellow Pages under cosmetics or skin care. Also listed there are representatives who will come to your home for makeup demonstrations.)

Personally, I like makeup that looks natural, but I've learned that putting on makeup is just like any other art. To look great takes a lot of time and practice and money. However, it's not necessary to spend a fortune on expensive brands, when drugstore varieties often work just as well. Better to initially spend a few dollars getting some professional advice on what to do and what to use, and then go shopping.

Check Out Hands and Feet

Proper care of hands and feet also embellishes our fashionable appearance. Cleanliness and upkeep are important.

I'll never pass the beautiful hands test, since I bite my fingernails. Still, weekly, I give myself a manicure and do the same to my feet. Where I live there are several shops that specialize in hand and foot care, and my friends who have the "works" tell me that it's a special treat. Recently, I had sculptured nails applied. They are expensive, but my morale improved 100% having glamorous hands for the first time in my life. They are difficult to maintain, but so are many beauty rituals such as coloring your hair. It's your decision as to what is important to you.

One of the tricks that fashion plays on its adoring public is always showing its wares off in the very finest setting. It isn't the size and shape of the model that makes the clothes look so great as much as it is the professional pizzazz that the model's appearance and presentation projects. Everything is perfect and brand new (no sagging hems, rundown shoes, mismatched accessories). Maybe we can't meet those standards every time, but we all can try HARDER.

So that's a quick rundown on "outside" maintenance, but what about our inner self? What fashionable homework can we do to shape up our self-esteem? Here are a few suggestions to give you an opportunity to experiment with special effects:

1. Purposely create an outfit that projects an image different from how you see yourself. Wear it for a day, and that evening make note of how the clothes that you wore affected your behavior and the others around you.
2. Take an outfit and change it at least three different ways. Did any version get more compliments than the others? Did you feel better in any one of the outfits? Why?
3. Wear colors that you haven't worn before. Did anyone notice? How did they make you feel?
4. Avoid wearing your present favorite color for a week in order to experiment with new colors. Did others mention any of the new colors?
5. Before going out, consider the occasion and create a "costume" that will say something about your personality, either by color or design. Did anyone get the message?

These simple tests will quickly demonstrate that the clothes that we wear affect our inner attitudes, as well as trigger other people's reaction toward us. We have to learn to trust, "to thine own self be true."

If I see myself as a "tailored" person, I won't feel comfortable in flamboyant ruffles. Wearing an outfit that I don't like and don't feel good in makes it impossible for me to project a positive impression. It's important to understand that, although we can use our clothes to create costumes and paint a smile on our face, we can't fool ourselves for long.

We need to look and dress in an appropriate manner, based on our own taste level. A fashionable appearance has to make us feel good before we can look good! In every instance in this book, I am encouraging you to ADAPT rather than IMITATE.

So many times we have been inhibited by our concern about size when, in reality, people we meet aren't as aware of our figures as they are intrigued by the message that we are broadcasting by our total appearance and attitude, which includes our mood, our posture, our dress and our manners.

What Message are You Broadcasting?

I am saying that I want to be a happy person. To accomplish that end, I've learned to be my own best friend, and I reward myself with Tender Loving Care, which may translate into a bubblebath or a smashing new outfit. I see that I need to be content with what and who I am today, instead of expecting future attainments or approval of others to satisfy my needs. One neat thing about being a NOW-PERSON is that we are set free from past behaviors and yesterday's concepts. Each day we write on a clean page, and we can be whoever and whatever we want to be, free to make changes, which is where fashion comes in to play.

Fashion is our helpmate! Fashion feeds on change, generating excitement. Fashion is definitely a feeling, and fooling around with it is FUN!

Christian Dior, the late French dress designer, described fashion as "something of the marvelous — something to take us away from our everyday lives."

Putting ourselves and our wardrobe into a fashionable framework is a very personal thing, but for whatever reasons we decide to act, our actions should give our life a visual and emotional boost.

Finally, we are free to do our own thing, now that we know how to SEW BIG!

The following isn't a complete listing of all the books that I used in researching SEW BIG, but they are books that I feel have special information that would be valuable for you to read.

Living in Portland, I had access to the Bassist Fashion Institute Library. I know that you don't have this privilege, so I tried to select books that you might find in your public library or in bookstores. The majority of them are available in paperback and can be inexpensively special ordered.

BOOKS

BREAKING ALL THE RULES...Feeling Good And Looking Great No Matter What Your Size, Nancy Roberts, VIKING PENGUIN In. New York

THE BIG BEAUTY BOOK, Glamour For The Fuller-Figure Woman, Ann Harper and Glenn Lewis, Holt, Rinehart and Winston, New York

SHORT CHIC, The Everything-You-Need-To-Know Fashion Guide For Every Woman Under 5' 4", Allison Kyle Leopold and Anne Marie Cloutier, Rawson/Wade, New York

BIG & BEAUTIFUL, How To Be Gorgeous On Your Own Grand Scale, Ruthanne Olds, Acropolis Books, Ltd., Washington, D.C.

LOOKING, WORKING, LIVING TERRIFIC 24 HOURS A DAY...Get Your Life In Order With Personal Style, Emily Cho and Hermine Leuders, G.P. Putnam Sons, New York

MICHAEL MARRON'S INSTANT MAKEOVER MAGIC, 150 Ways To Improve Your Makeup, Hair, Dress, Body Language And More In Record Time, Rawson Associates, New York

MOTHER PLETSCH'S PAINLESS SEWING, Pati Palmer and Susan Pletsch, Palmer & Pletsch Assoc., Portland, Oregon

CHAPTER 14

Fashion Bibliography

VIDEOS

SEWING WITH NANCY...SEWING THAT FITS...Fashion That Fits No Matter What The Size, Nancy Zieman, contact Nancy's Notions Sewing Catalog, P.O. Box 683, Beaver Dam, WI 53916.

PERIODICALS

W, A WEEKLY NEWSPAPER PUBLISHED BY FAIRCHILD PUBLICATIONS (write Subscription Service, P.O. Box 595, Hightown, N.J., for information), features the best of the editorial material from *Women's Wear Daily*.

VOGUE or McCALL'S PATTERNS, VOGUE, HARPERS, GLAMOUR MAGAZINE, MADEMOISELLE and *BIG, BEAUTIFUL WOMAN* all have something to say each month. Choose several.

More Products from Palmer/Pletsch

Look for these Palmer/Pletsch easy-to-use, information-filled sewing books and videos in local fabric stores, or contact us for ordering information.

☐ **The Serger Idea Book—A Collection of Inspiring Ideas from Palmer/Pletsch,** Color photos and how-to's on inspiring and fashionable ideas from the Extraordinary to the Practical. *8½×11, 160 pgs., $18.95*

Books available spiral bound— add $3.00 for large books, $2.00 for small.

☐ **Creative Serging for the Home and Other Quick Decorating Ideas,** by *Lynette Ranney Black and Linda Wisner.* Color photos and how-to's to help you transform your home into the place you want it to be. *8½×11, 160 pgs., $18.95*

☐ **Sewing Ultrasuede Brand Products** by *Marta Alto, Pati Palmer and Barbara Weiland.* Fashion photo section, plus the newest techniques to master these luxurious fabrics. *8½×11, 128 pgs., $18.95*

☐ **Sewing With Sergers—The Complete Handbook for Overlock Sewing,** by *Pati Palmer and Gail Brown.* Learn easy threading tips, stitch types, rolled edging and flatlocking on your serger. *128 pgs., $6.95*

☐ **Creative Serging—The Complete Handbook for Decorative Overlock Sewing,** by *Pati Palmer, Gail Brown and Sue Green.* In-depth information and creative uses of your serger. *128 pgs., $6.95 (Not available in spiral)*

☐ **Creative Serging Illustrated,** Same as Creative Serging PLUS color photography. *160 pgs., $14.95 (Not available in spiral)*

☐ **Sew to Success!—How to Make Money in a Home-Based Sewing Business,** by *Kathleen Spike.* Learn how to establish your market, set policies and procedures, price your talents and more! *128 pgs., $10.95*

☐ **Mother Pletsch's Painless Sewing,** *Revised Edition,* by *Pati Palmer and Susan Pletsch.* The most uncomplicated sewing book of the century! Filled with sewing tips on how to sew FAST! *128 pgs., $8.95*

☐ **Sensational Silk—A Handbook for Sewing Silk and Silk-like Fabrics,** by *Gail Brown.* Complete guide for sewing with silkies from selection to perfection in sewing. *128 pgs., $6.95*

☐ **Easy, Easier, Easiest Tailoring,** *Revised Edition,* by *Pati Palmer and Susan Pletsch.* Learn 4 different tailoring methods, easy fit tips, and timesaving machine lining. *128 pgs., $6.95*

☐ **Pants For Any Body,** *Revised Edition,* by *Pati Palmer and Susan Pletsch.* Learn to fit pants with clear step-by-step problem and solution illustrations. *128 pgs., $6.95*

☐ **Clothes Sense—Straight Talk About Wardrobe Planning,** by *Barbara Weiland and Leslie Wood.* Learn to define your personal style and when to sew or buy. *128 pgs., $6.95*

☐ **Sew a Beautiful Wedding,** by *Gail Brown and Karen Dillon.* Bridal how-to's on choosing the most flattering style to sewing with specialty fabrics. *128 pgs., $6.95*

☐ **Couture Sewing,** by *Roberta Carr.* Coming March 1992.

VIDEOS— *$29.95 each* (VHS only)
☐ **Sewing the Time Saving Way** *(45 min.)*
☐ **Sewing to Success** *(45 min.)*
☐ **Sewing With Sergers — Basics** *(1 hr.)*
☐ **Sewing With Sergers — Advanced** *(1 hr.)*
☐ **Creative Serging** *(1 hr.)*
☐ **Creative Serging II** *(1 hr.)*
☐ **Sewing with Ultrasuede** *(1 hr.)*

We also publish a series of **Trends Bulletins**, and carry hard-to-find and unique threads (Decor 6 Rayon, Woolly Nylon, Candlelight metallic threads—order our color cards for $2), notions, and **Henckels sewing scissors**. If not available at a store near you, write for more information.

Palmer Pletsch Associates
P.O. Box 12046
Portland, OR 97212
(503) 274-0687

International orders please pay in U.S. funds or with Visa or MasterCard. Shipping and handling: ($1–13.99) $1.75; ($14–24) $2.00; ($25–29.99) $3.00; ($50+) $4.00. Please allow 4–6 weeks for delivery.